God's Attributes

Making HIM Known

God's Attributes

BY JILL NELSON

P&R

PUBLISHING

P.O. BOX 817 • PHILLIPSBURG • NEW JERSEY 08865-0817

Library of Congress Cataloging-in-Publication Data

Names: Nelson, Jill, 1960- author. | Apps, Fred, illustrator.
Title: God's attributes / Jill Nelson ; [illustrations by Fred Apps]
Description: Phillipsburg, New Jersey : P&R Publishing Company, 2022. |
   Series: Making him known | Summary: "Introduce your children to God's
   holiness, goodness, love, and more with this interactive family
   devotional. Each entry explores one of God's attributes, encouraging
   readers to take these truths to heart"-- Provided by publisher.
Identifiers: LCCN 2021029403 | ISBN 9781629958903 (paperback) | ISBN
   9781629958910 (epub)
Subjects: LCSH: God (Christianity)--Attributes--Juvenile literature.
Classification: LCC BT130 .N45 2022 | DDC 231/.4--dc23
LC record available at https://lccn.loc.gov/2021029403

For my granddaughter,
Elizabeth Marie House

May the words of this book help you to see
the incomparable greatness and worth of God.
Through Christ, may you experience God as your
greatest treasure and your all-satisfying joy.
May you trust, love, and follow Him all
the days of your life!

I will extol you, my God and King,
and bless your name forever and ever.
Every day I will bless you
and praise your name forever and ever.
Great is the LORD, and greatly to be praised,
and his greatness is unsearchable.
—Psalm 145:1–3

Contents

Preface

Every day, children are full of a myriad of questions. They have a God-given curiosity to know the "who, what, where, when, and why" of everything around them. Discovering answers is how they grow in knowledge and understanding. But some questions tower above all others in importance. As adults, we have the sacred responsibility to direct them to the most essential questions of all: Who is God? What is He like? How should I act toward God?

God's Attributes has been written to address these questions. In looking at God's Word, children will be led to discover the incomparable beauty and grandeur of the greatness and worth of God. It's important to note that there is a strategic flow to the chapters that is meant to lead to a clear presentation of the gospel. Through this structure, children can better understand the essence, means, and goal of the gospel within the larger context of God's character.

May this book serve as a tool by which the Holy Spirit would be pleased to awaken hearts and cause children to grow in their capacity to be absolutely stunned beyond measure by the one true God. May our children, like Paul, come to say with wholehearted conviction,

> Indeed, I count everything as loss because of the surpassing worth of knowing Christ Jesus my Lord. (Philippians 3:8)

Introduction
How to Use This Book

This book was written to give parents an opportunity to present solid truth to their children and to encourage real-life application of that truth.

Relational

Children receive more encouragement to learn when truth is presented by a trusted individual. Your positive, relational parent-child commitment will be a real benefit when you sit down together to read this book. Your time together over the Word should be positive, affirming, and loving.

Interactive

There is a greater impact when an individual *discovers* truth instead of just hearing it presented. Many questions have been incorporated into the text of this book to encourage your child to wonder and think critically. The process of discovery will be circumvented if you don't give your child adequate time to think and respond. After asking a question, wait for a response. If your child has difficulty, ask the question in a different way or give a few hints.

Questions and responses can be springboards for more questions and discovery as you interact with your child's mind and heart. The Holy Spirit is the real teacher, so depend on Him to give both you and your child thoughts and truths to explore together, and to bring the necessary understanding. Take the time to work through each story at a leisurely pace—giving time for interaction and further dialogue. The goal should be to get the material into the child, not just to get the child through the material.

Understandable

These stories have been written with attention given to explaining difficult or potentially new concepts. Some of these concepts may take time for your child to digest. Allow your child to ponder new truths. Read the story more than once, allowing the truth to be better understood and integrated into your child's theological framework. At times, have your child read parts of the lesson, giving an opportunity for visual learning.

Because vocabulary can be child-specific, define the particular words foreign to your child. Retell difficult sections in familiar wording, and ask questions to be sure your child understands the truth being taught. Note that most chapters focus on a particular attribute of God. Each is highlighted in ALL CAPS and followed by a child-friendly definition. For example, "God is INCOMPREHENSIBLE—God is more than we can fully understand."

Theological

More than just acquainting your child with an understanding of some distinct attributes of God, this book is building a foundation of biblical theology for your child. As your child begins to correctly understand who God is and how He interacts with the world, he or she won't have just a vague notion of God, but will be able to relate to the God of the Bible.

Because the Word of God has convicting and converting power, Bible texts are quoted word for word in some parts. Some of these verses may be beyond the child's understanding, so you may want to explain unfamiliar words or thoughts. Even though clear comprehension may be difficult, hearing the Word itself is a means that the Holy Spirit often uses to encourage faith in your child (Romans 10:17). Do not minimize the effectual influence of God's Word in the tender souls of children.

Since the Word of God is living and active, allow the child to read the actual Bible verses as much as possible. Also, encourage your child to memorize some of the verses so he or she can meditate on them at other times.

The gospel is presented numerous times throughout the book. Use this as an opportunity to share God's work of grace in your life, and to converse with your child about his or her spiritual condition. Be careful not to confuse spiritual interest with converting faith, and take care to avoid giving premature assurances. Fan the flames of gospel-inspired conviction and tenderness toward the sacrificial love of Jesus without prematurely encouraging your child to pray "the sinner's prayer."[1]

Application

Understanding the truth is essential, but understanding alone is insufficient. Truth must also be embraced in the heart and acted upon in daily life. Often, children cannot make the connection between a biblical truth and real-life application, so you, the parent, must help bridge the gap.

Consider the following quotation by D. Martyn Lloyd-Jones:

> We must always put things in the right order, and it is Truth first. . . . The heart is always to be influenced through the understanding—the mind, then the heart, then the will. . . . But God forbid that anyone should think that it ends with the intellect. It starts there, but it goes on. It then moves the heart and finally the man yields his will. He obeys, not grudgingly or unwillingly, but with the whole heart. The Christian life is a glorious perfect life that takes up and captivates the entire personality.[2]

Spend a few days or even a week on each story. Reread the story, discuss the truths, and follow the suggestions in the Learning to Trust God section. Most importantly, help your child to see that God is who He says He is, and help him

---

1. Some excellent resources for parents regarding the salvation of children can be found at www.truth78.org, including a booklet titled *Helping Children to Understand the Gospel*.
2. D. Martyn Lloyd-Jones, *Spiritual Depression* (Grand Rapids: William B. Eerdmans, 1965), 61–62.

or her to act in response to the truth. Point out God's involvement in daily life and thank Him for being true to His Word.

Prayer

Ultimately, our efforts are effective only if the Holy Spirit breathes on our teaching and quickens it to the heart. Pray not only before going through the stories, but also in the succeeding days, that your child would see the incomparable greatness and worth of God and experience Him as his or her greatest treasure through faith in Christ.

The Most Important Questions

Have you ever thought about how many questions we ask every day? Questions like, "When are we going to the park? Where did I leave my book? How long until dinner? Why do I have to clean my room? What happened to the television? Who is our new neighbor?" . . . and on and on. Why so many questions? Because we are curious and want to know things—especially things that matter to us.

Of course, some questions are more important than others. For instance, "Can the doctor help Grandma get well?" is much more important than "What can I have for a snack?" But did you know that there are certain questions that are more important than *any* others? They are the MOST important questions in the whole world—the most important questions for every person, no matter how young or old they are or where they live. Questions like . . .

Who is God, but the LORD? (2 Samuel 22:32)

Who is like you, O LORD, among the gods?
　　Who is like you, majestic in holiness,
　　awesome in glorious deeds, doing wonders? (Exodus 15:11)

What are these questions asking? We could say that they ask two main things: *Who is God?* and *What is God like?*

These two short questions are the MOST important questions of all! How can that be? They are most important because their answers matter more than anything else.

Where would you find the answers to these two most important questions? God Himself tells us:

The unfolding of [God's] words gives light;
    it imparts understanding. (Psalm 119:130)

Every word of God proves true. (Proverbs 30:5)

All Scripture is breathed out by God. (2 Timothy 3:16)

Where can you find the answers to these most important questions? In the Bible! God has given us the Bible so that we can know and understand who God is and what He is like. Yes, your dad and mom and others have probably taught you true answers about who God is and what God is like, but those true answers came from the Bible. There is no other book like the Bible. Because it is God's own words, it tells the absolute TRUTH—and it tells us the truth about God. For example, in the Bible, God says,

I am God, and there is no other;
I am God, and there is none like me. (Isaiah 46:9)

Who is God? He tells us the answer: "I am God, and there is no other." The God of the Bible is the one and only God. *What is God like?* "There is none like me." That means that no one and nothing else can compare to God. He is one of a kind. God is so different and special; He is like nothing else.

But do you think that this one Bible verse *completely* answers the two most important questions? Does it answer *everything* that God wants us to know about who He is and what He is like? Of course not. We know this because the Bible is filled with thousands upon thousands of verses that tell us more wonderful, exciting, and awesome things about God!

But there is another MOST important question to ask after "Who is God?" and "What is God like?" What is it? Before guessing, imagine for a moment that you are playing outside and you see a brilliant flash of lightning and hear a huge clap of thunder. Next, the wind blows so hard that the trees begin to sway and rain starts to pour down. How might you respond? Why might one kind of response lead to safety and another kind of response lead to danger? There are right and wrong ways to act toward a thunderstorm. Now can you guess what the third most important question might be?

How should I act toward God?

Because there is only one true God and because He is more spectacular than a thunderstorm or anything else, there are certain ways you should act toward Him—right and wrong ways to respond. You don't need to guess what these are because, just as the Bible tells us the truth about who God is and what He is like, the Bible also tells us the truth about how all people should act toward God. Here is just one example:

You shall love the LORD your God with all your heart and with all your soul and with all your might. (Deuteronomy 6:5)

In this book, we will be going on a kind of treasure hunt through God's Word looking for answers to the questions *Who is God? What is God like?* and *How should I act toward God?* The answers are meant to amaze you beyond anything you could ever imagine and give you hope, comfort, strength, peace, and more happiness than you ever thought you could have! In fact, learning the answers about who God is, what He is like, and how you should act toward Him are meant to lead you to find life and joy forever and ever!

LEARNING TO TRUST GOD

✤ Read 2 Samuel 22:32 and Exodus 15:11 again. Do you see any special words in these verses that hint at or tell you something about who God is and what He is like? Read Deuteronomy 6:5 again. Why would this be a right response to God? Is that the way you respond to God? Can you think of other right ways to respond to God?

✤ Read 2 Timothy 3:14–17. Why is knowing the Bible so important? What does the Bible "make you wise for"? How does verse 15 answer the question "How should I act toward God?" Why is this more important than anything else?

✤ *Activity:* Take about ten minutes to make a list of things you already know about God—special words that describe who God is and what He is like. How would a person check your answers to see if they are correct? What is one way you could rightly respond to God this week?

God Is Incomprehensible

Have you ever been asked a question that you couldn't answer? Maybe it was a difficult question on a math assignment, and you had no idea how to answer it. Or maybe your mom asked where you put your jacket, and you couldn't remember. How do you feel when you don't know the answers?

Now think back to the most important questions of all: Who is God? What is God like? How should I act toward God? The answers to these questions are more important than anything else and are found in the Bible. But do you think a person could find out *everything* there is to know about God? Could you? Could your parents? Your pastor? How about a famous person from the Bible? Let's look at an example.

A man named Job lived a long, long time ago. His story is written in a book of the Old Testament called Job, and it begins by telling us about Job's life. Job had a wife and ten children, whom he loved very much. He also owned thousands of animals, which meant he was very rich. But most importantly, Job was "blameless and upright, one who feared God and turned away from evil" (Job 1:1). Job knew and loved God!

However, one day things started to go terribly wrong. First, all Job's animals were killed, so his riches were lost. Next, all ten of his children died—how horribly sad! Then Job got very sick with painful sores all over his body. Someone might ask, Why did all these bad things happen to Job? Had Job done something to make God angry? Was God being unfair? Couldn't God stop these bad things from happening?

During this sad time, three of Job's friends came to visit him. They thought they knew the answers about what was happening to Job. They thought they had the answers about who God is, what He is like, and why Job was suffering. But

Job didn't agree with his friends, and they argued back and forth. Finally, one of Job's friends said this:

God thunders wondrously with his voice;
  he does great things that we cannot comprehend. (Job 37:5)

What did Job's friend mean by saying that God "does great things that we cannot comprehend"? It means that God does things that we cannot completely understand. God does things that are too mysterious for us to fully understand. In other words, no one can completely and fully know *everything* about who God is and what He is like.

Even after Job's friend said that, Job and his friends kept arguing. Finally, the only One who does know God completely and fully answered Job. Can you guess who that was? God Himself. But He had a different way of answering Job. God answered Job by asking him lots and lots of questions like . . .

Where were you when I laid the foundation of the earth? (Job 38:4)

Can you send forth lightnings? (Job 38:35)

Do you give the horse his might? (Job 39:19)

Is it by your understanding that the hawk soars? (Job 39:26)

Have you an arm like God,
    and can you thunder with a voice like his? (Job 40:9)

On and on God questioned Job like this. Why do you think God asked Job these kinds of questions? Do you think Job came away feeling really smart and proud of his knowledge of God? No! Here is how Job responded:

I have uttered what I did not understand,
    things too wonderful for me, which I did not know. (Job 42:3)

Job also said to God that he was very sorry because he now realized that God is too great and wonderful to completely and fully comprehend.

God is INCOMPREHENSIBLE—God is more than we can fully understand.

Like Job, we will never fully know and understand all the answers about who God is and what He is like. No matter how old you are or how many times you read and study the Bible, there will always be more and more exciting things to learn about the greatness of God. Imagine finding a giant treasure chest filled with dazzling jewels and gold. You eagerly begin to remove and admire each treasure but find that the treasure chest never empties—there are always more and more wonders to discover inside. The incomprehensible God is millions of times more dazzling! Every day there are new riches to discover about God.

Oh, the depth of the riches and wisdom and knowledge of God! How unsearchable are his judgments and how inscrutable his ways! (Romans 11:33)

But there is one more question we need to ask: Because God is incomprehensible, how should we act toward Him? What is the right way to respond to a God who is more than we can fully understand? We should be humble before Him and praise Him for his greatness!

> Every day I will bless you
> > and praise your name forever and ever.
> Great is the LORD, and greatly to be praised,
> > and his greatness is unsearchable. (Psalm 145:2–3)

LEARNING TO TRUST GOD

✤ Are there things about God that you have a hard time fully understanding? Even though God is incomprehensible, He makes us able to understand enough about Himself so that we can truly know, love, and trust Him. Read and talk about 1 Corinthians 2:12 and John 20:31.

✤ Reread Job's response to God's questions. What kind of attitude does it show? Why is being humble a right way to act toward God? Why is this attitude especially important when things happen that we don't fully understand? Review Job 37:5 and Romans 11:33.

✤ *Activity:* With your parents, talk about ways you can learn more about God this week. Here are some ideas: make a daily plan to read the Bible, memorize one or more verses, or take sermon notes.

God Is Eternal

How many birthdays have you celebrated? What are some of your favorite things to do on your birthday?

Why are birthdays so special? They are special because we are remembering and celebrating a brand-new life that came into the world—yours! But did you know that you actually came into *existence*—your life started—before your birthday? You had your true beginning the very first moment you began to grow inside your mother. Every person has a beginning. Before your beginning, you didn't exist.

But what about the one true God? Did He have a beginning? What age is God? Does He have a birthday? Where would you find the answers? Yes, in the Bible.

> Your throne is established from of old;
> you are from everlasting. (Psalm 93:2)

This verse uses the word *old* to explain how long God has ruled the world. But does it give us a number of years—one hundred, one thousand, or even one million years? No, it doesn't. Instead, it uses another word to describe how old God is. God is from *everlasting*. That means God had no beginning. He has always existed. Unlike everything and everyone else, God has no birthday.

> Before the mountains were brought forth,
> or ever you had formed the earth and the world,
> from everlasting to everlasting you are God. (Psalm 90:2)

Compared to us, mountains are really old, and so is the earth. In fact, they are thousands of years old. The God who is "from everlasting" created them. They had a beginning, a moment when they were brought into existence by God. But this verse also points to another important thing about God. God is not only "from everlasting." He is also "to everlasting." What does that mean? It means that God will have no ending. He alone has always existed—always been—and will never go out of existence. In the Bible, there is a word that describes this truth about God:

The eternal God is your dwelling place. (Deuteronomy 33:27)

God is ETERNAL—God has no beginning or end.

Think about this: God didn't simply pop into being a long, long time ago. He was never created. God, and God alone, has always existed. Imagine traveling back in time millions of years, or even zillions upon zillions of years before

anything else existed. God would be there. He is the eternal God! That is truly *incomprehensible.*

Pictures or symbols can sometimes help us to better understand true things about God. Find the circle on this page. Can you see a starting point where the circle began? No. Can you see an ending point? No. This can help us to see what it means that God is eternal. God had no starting point (no beginning) and has no ending point (no end).

Why is it important to know that God is eternal? Read each verse and answer the questions that follow:

> But the LORD is the true God;
>> he is the living God and the everlasting King. (Jeremiah 10:10)

Is God alive right now? Will God still be God a billion years from now? How long will God remain King over all?

> The LORD is the everlasting God,
>> the Creator of the ends of the earth.
> He does not faint or grow weary;
>> his understanding is unsearchable. (Isaiah 40:28)

Will the eternal God ever get tired, worn out, or weak?

> But the steadfast love of the LORD is from everlasting to everlasting on
>> those who fear him. (Psalm 103:17)

How long will God's love for His people last?

Do you see why it really matters that God is eternal? What difference should this make in your life? Because God is eternal, how should you act toward Him?

"Trust in the LORD forever, for the LORD GOD is an everlasting rock" (Isaiah 26:4). This verse describes the Lord God as an "everlasting rock." Think about a huge, flat rock for a minute. It is firm, heavy, and long-lasting. You can depend on it to hold you and not crumble underneath you. Now picture God as a kind of *everlasting* rock. God is *always and forever* dependable. We can "trust in the LORD forever" and be confident that God will *always and forever* rule over His world. You can be sure that He will *always and forever* love and take care of His people. When He says something, you can *always and forever* depend on it to happen just as He says. Trust in God to *always and forever* keep His promises, including this amazing promise:

> For God so loved the world, that he gave his only Son, that whoever believes in him should not perish but have eternal life. (John 3:16)

LEARNING TO TRUST GOD

✦ What is a "dwelling place"? Why do we need things like houses? Do houses last forever? Why not? Now read Deuteronomy 33:27 again. Why is it important to know that God is an eternal dwelling place for His people? How does a person enter this dwelling place? Read John 3:16 again.

✦ Have you ever been disappointed by something that didn't last? Maybe something broke, got used up, or was lost. Maybe a friend moved away or a pet died. Will the eternal God ever prove to be disappointing in these ways? Why not?

✦ *Activity:* At the top of a sheet of drawing paper, write the words "Trust in the LORD forever, for the LORD GOD is an . . ." Below this, draw a picture of yourself standing on a giant rock. Inside the rock, write the words ". . . everlasting rock" (Isaiah 26:4).

God Is Glorious

Have you ever heard of something called show-and-tell? It's a classroom activity in which students bring something special from home to show while they tell the class about it. Suppose a girl brought a fancy jewelry box for show-and-tell. She described the glittering, colorful gems inside. But she never actually opened the jewelry box to show the class what was inside. What might the class begin to wonder?

Why does the *show* part matter? Because it provides proof of the *tell* part.

Now think of the Bible. The Bible is filled with God's words—words that always tell the truth about who God is and what God is like. For example, the Bible tells us that God is eternal, as we saw in the last chapter. But is there anything that actually *shows* that the things the Bible says are true? Does God show us who He is and what He is like in a way we can see?

> His invisible attributes, namely, his eternal power and divine nature, have been clearly perceived, ever since the creation of the world, in the things that have been made. (Romans 1:20)

This verse first tells us that there is something "invisible"—something unseen. What is it? God's "attributes." What are attributes? These are qualities or characteristics that God has. They describe who God is and what He is like. God's "eternal power and divine nature" are attributes of God. They tell us something of His greatness and worth. But notice the very next thing the verse tells us: God's invisible attributes "have been clearly perceived" (which means seen). How can they be both invisible AND clearly seen? What is the answer? God's attributes can be clearly seen in and through the things He has made.

Take a minute to look out a window if you can and name all the things you see. Or list all the yummy foods you have enjoyed this week. All these created things are showing you a glimpse of God's greatness and worth!

So when you see a dog playing and running after a ball, God is showing you a little bit of His own happiness. When you bite into a yummy apple, God is showing you a little bit of His goodness. When you hear the rumbling of thunder, God is showing you a little bit of His great power. Flowers, waves, mountains, volcanoes, waterfalls, birds, giraffes, elephants, trees, bananas, clouds, lightning, snow, and all the millions of things God has created show us a glimpse of His greatness and worth. God's creation is His own show-and-tell!

The heavens declare the glory of God,
    and the sky above proclaims his handiwork.
Day to day pours out speech,
    and night to night reveals knowledge. (Psalm 19:1–2)

God is GLORIOUS—He shows His greatness and worth.

But God doesn't just show us His greatness and worth through what He has created. He shows us His glory by what He has done—His deeds. Here is a song that the people of Israel sang after God had done something amazing for them. See if you can guess what God had done.

> I will sing to the LORD, for he has triumphed gloriously;
>> the horse and his rider he has thrown into the sea. (Exodus 15:1)

> Who is like you, majestic in holiness,
>> awesome in glorious deeds, doing wonders? (Exodus 15:11)

What had the Lord just done for Israel? He had freed them from captivity in Egypt. God miraculously parted a sea so that His people could walk to safety. But the Egyptian armies followed Israel to bring them back to Egypt. So once Israel was safely across the sea, God returned the sea waters and "covered" the Egyptians—destroying them completely. God didn't just *tell* Israel about His power and love for them; He *showed* them. All of Israel saw a glimpse of the greatness and worth of God that day. God's deeds are truly glorious!

God is glorious in everything He does, whether it is creating the world, creating people to fill the world, choosing a people for Himself, parting the sea, or destroying an enemy. The eternal God is still glorious today. Everywhere we go, and in every situation, we should be looking to see glimpses of God's glory . . . while getting hugs from our parents, enjoying our favorite desserts, hearing birds sing, playing with friends, watching powerful storms, and petting furry puppies.

> Blessed be his glorious name forever;
>> may the whole earth be filled with his glory! (Psalm 72:19)

Most importantly, God showed the world His glory when He gave up His Son to die on the cross for sinners. Now you see His glory when He causes a heart to trust in Jesus, answers a prayer, gives you strength to obey even when it's hard, provides comfort when you hurt, and brings His people to heaven. God's glory in all these things is far beyond the greatness and worth of any treasure you could ever imagine! So how should you act toward this glorious God?

> Shout for joy to God, all the earth;
>> sing the glory of his name;
>> give to him glorious praise!
> Say to God, "How awesome are your deeds!" (Psalm 66:1–3)

LEARNING TO TRUST GOD

✣ Take a few minutes and see how many glorious deeds of God you can recall from the Bible. Now think of some glorious deeds God has done in your church, your family, and your own life. How should you respond to these deeds? Read and talk about Psalm 145:1–6. How can you put these verses into action this week?

✣ Recall some of the most amazing, awesome, and spectacular things you have seen. Why did you find them so "glorious" (great and valuable)? How do they compare with the glory of God? What makes God's greatness and worth beyond compare?

✣ *Activity:* Go on a nature walk, or even a walk around your yard. Carefully look for and keep count of how many different things God has created in just that little space on earth. (Be sure to also look up at the sky.) Then have your parents help you to choose a song to sing in praise to God.

God Is Wise

Have you ever put a puzzle together? If you did, how many pieces were there? What did the finished puzzle look like? Puzzles are interesting things. They are made by joining together hundreds of specially shaped pieces in just the right way. Every piece is needed to complete the picture.

Now try to imagine a *giant* puzzle—one so big that it would fill the earth, the sky, and outer space, made of billions upon billions of pieces, more pieces than you could possibly count! Would you be surprised to know that there really *is* a kind of puzzle this big?

In the beginning, God created the heavens and the earth. (Genesis 1:1)

God's creation is like a giant puzzle. God has specially designed and shaped each piece of His creation—billions and billions of things—to fit together perfectly. Here is a tiny example:

You make springs gush forth in the valleys;
    they flow between the hills;
they give drink to every beast of the field;
    the wild donkeys quench their thirst.
Beside them the birds of the heavens dwell;
    they sing among the branches. (Psalm 104:10–12)

You cause the grass to grow for the livestock
    and plants for man to cultivate,
that he may bring forth food from the earth. (Psalm 104:14)

How many "pieces" of God's creation do you see in these verses? How do they work together? Read the second quote from Psalm 104 again and think about this: God made the earth's soil to provide a good place for seeds to sprout. God made the sun to give energy for plants to grow. God made rain to water plants. God created bees to pollinate flowers so that plants can produce all kinds of delicious foods. God created man with the ability to plant and harvest food. Every piece of God's creation is wonderfully designed, even the tiniest things. How was God able to create such a marvelous world?

> O LORD, how manifold are your works!
>> In wisdom have you made them all. (Psalm 104:24)

> The LORD by wisdom founded the earth;
>> by understanding he established the heavens. (Proverbs 3:19)

God made everything in and by *wisdom*. That means that the eternal God created all things according to a glorious plan. He knew how to design and create everything to fit and work together perfectly in order to finish that plan.

God is WISE—He causes everything to work out perfectly.

But God's wisdom goes beyond His creation of the heavens and earth. God's wisdom is also seen in all the ways He acts in the world and especially in how He acts in the lives of His people. Let's look at an example of that. The story is found in the book of Genesis.

God promised to make a man named Jacob and his twelve sons into a great nation called Israel. They were to be God's specially chosen people. God planned to bless the whole world through Israel (Genesis 28:13–14).

Jacob's favorite son was Joseph. Joseph had interesting dreams. In one of his dreams, Joseph saw himself in a position of power over his father and brothers. This made his brothers so angry that they felt like killing him! Instead, they decided to sell Joseph as a slave, and he was taken far away to the land of Egypt. To cover up what they did, the brothers told Jacob that Joseph had been killed by a fierce animal (Genesis 37).

While Joseph was a slave in Egypt, God was with him. Joseph did his work so well that he was soon put in charge of many things. But one day he was thrown in prison, even though he had done nothing wrong (Genesis 39). After a while, a strange thing happened: Joseph was sent to meet with Pharaoh, the king of Egypt. Why? Pharaoh had heard that Joseph could interpret dreams. Pharaoh told Joseph about a dream he had, and, sure enough, Joseph was able to explain it. He told Pharaoh that there would be seven years with plenty of food in Egypt followed by seven years of famine. People would need to store up food during the first seven years to survive the famine. Pharaoh decided to put Joseph in charge of doing this (Genesis 41).

The famine didn't come only to Egypt; Joseph's father and brothers also didn't have enough to eat. God's special people, Israel, were in danger of starving, so Jacob sent his sons to Egypt to buy food. There they discovered that Joseph was alive and had become a very important man. God brought Joseph and his family back together. Joseph forgave his brothers and gave them all the food they needed. God's special people were saved and went on to bless the whole world (Genesis 42–46).

There are so many different "pieces" to this story. Did some pieces seem like they didn't fit into God's plan to make Israel a great nation? But God knew exactly what He was doing. From the very beginning, God planned to save His people by sending Joseph to Egypt. Nothing happened by chance. Even the "bad" parts were meant to complete God's plan. Remember, God is WISE—He causes everything to work out perfectly. It was true back then, and it will be true always and forever. Knowing this, how should *you* act toward God?

> Trust in the LORD with all your heart,
>> and do not lean on your own understanding. (Proverbs 3:5)

LEARNING TO TRUST GOD

✦ What events in God's plan to save Israel seemed out of place? How did God cause those events to work together to complete His plan? Read Proverbs 3:5–7. Do you have a hard time trusting in God's wise plans? Why is this difficult at times? What would help you to trust God?

✦ Some of God's attributes belong to Him alone. For example, only God is eternal. But God chooses to share some of His attributes with people. Read Proverbs 2:6. What does God want to give you? How do you get it? (See Psalm 19:7; Matthew 7:24; and James 1:5.)

✦ *Activity:* Make a "God's Wisdom in Creation" puzzle. Find a picture (perhaps from an old calendar) that shows something wonderful in God's creation. Cut it up into different shaped puzzle pieces. Mix up the pieces, and then see how quickly you can put it together again. Review Psalm 104:24.

God Is Almighty

What is the heaviest thing you have ever lifted? How long were you able to lift it? Will you get stronger as you grow older? Is there a *limit* to what a person can lift—a point where he or she can't lift anything heavier? Even the world's strongest men have a limit to their strength. That is why people build powerful machines like cranes and bulldozers to lift or move really heavy things. But machines also have a limit to their strength. Do you think God has a limit to His strength?

> Lift up your eyes on high and see:
>> who created these?
> He who brings out their host by number,
>> calling them all by name;
> by the greatness of his might
>> and because he is strong in power,
>> not one is missing. (Isaiah 40:26)

When you look up in the sky on a dark and cloudless night, what do you see? A "host" of stars. God created billions of stars. Even though they appear very tiny, each one is actually enormous in size—much bigger and heavier than the earth! What keeps them up in the heavens? Why don't they fall to earth? Because of the greatness of God's might, strength, and power! Exactly how powerful is God?

> Ah, Lord GOD! It is you who have made the heavens and the earth by your great power and by your outstretched arm! Nothing is too hard for you. (Jeremiah 32:17)

I am God Almighty. (Genesis 17:1)

Is anything too hard for God? Does He have any limit on His strength or power? No. That is why He calls Himself "God Almighty."

God is ALMIGHTY—He is all-powerful. God is mightier, stronger, and more powerful than anything or anyone else. His great power has no limit at all!

God's almighty power is important for making sure His plans work out perfectly. Remember the story of Israel and Joseph from the last chapter? God had made a very special promise to make Israel into a great nation. In His wisdom, God had sent Joseph to Egypt so that Israel would be saved from a famine. After the famine, God's people lived in Egypt for hundreds of years. During that time, the Israelites "multiplied and grew exceedingly strong" (Exodus 1:7). The new Pharaoh of Egypt became worried, thinking the Israelites would become rivals—competitors—for his power. So the Egyptians "ruthlessly made the people of Israel work as slaves" (Exodus 1:13). Not surprisingly, "the people of Israel groaned . . . and cried out for help" (Exodus 2:23). God Almighty heard their cries and chose a leader for Israel, a man named Moses. God said to Moses,

Now, behold, the cry of the people of Israel has come to me, and I have also seen the oppression with which the Egyptians oppress them. Come,

I will send you to Pharaoh that you may bring my people, the children of Israel, out of Egypt. (Exodus 3:9–10)

Imagine having to tell the mighty Pharaoh that God wanted His people to go free. That's scary to think about. But Moses obeyed God and, along with his brother, Aaron, went to Pharaoh and said,

"Thus says the LORD, the God of Israel, 'Let my people go . . .'"
But Pharaoh said, "Who is the LORD, that I should obey his voice and let Israel go? I do not know the LORD, and moreover, I will not let Israel go." (Exodus 5:1–2)

Who is stronger—the Lord God or Pharaoh and his armies? This is what God said in response:

The Egyptians shall know that I am the LORD, when I stretch out my hand against Egypt and bring out the people of Israel from among them. (Exodus 7:5)

What happened when the almighty God stretched out His hand? Ten different plagues—terrible disasters—came upon the Egyptians: the Nile river turned to blood; swarms of frogs, gnats, and flies covered the land; livestock died; skin sores covered men and beasts; then came hail, locusts, and total darkness; and lastly all the firstborn of Egypt died! Finally, Pharaoh let God's people go.

But why did it take so many plagues? Couldn't God have defeated the Egyptians after just one plague? Did it take God ten tries to defeat Pharaoh? Here is what God told Pharaoh:

For by now I could have put out my hand and struck you and your people with pestilence, and you would have been cut off from the earth. But for this purpose I have raised you up, to show you my power, so that my name may be proclaimed in all the earth. (Exodus 9:15–16)

Suppose you saw a man lift a car over his head. Unbelievable! But what if he lifted ten cars! Wow! He would be famous all over the world! Yes, almighty God could have easily defeated Pharaoh with just one plague. But ten plagues proved God *even more* powerful and caused His fame to spread throughout the world. He is the one true almighty God!

One generation shall commend your works to another,
    and shall declare your mighty acts. (Psalm 145:4)

They shall speak of the might of your awesome deeds,
    and I will declare your greatness. (Psalm 145:6)

LEARNING TO TRUST GOD

✦ Where have you seen God's power on display this week? Why is God's power bad news for people who try to fight against Him? Why is it good news for people who love and trust Him? (See verses such as Psalm 27:1–2; Isaiah 41:10; John 10:27–29; Romans 8:31, 38–39; and 1 Corinthians 6:14.)

✦ When you see something powerful like a flash of lightning, what is your response? Would it be a good idea to run out and try to touch it? Why not? How does the power of lightning compare to the power of God? What should your attitude be toward His power? Read Psalm 111:10.

✦ *Activity:* Have your parents help you to find the words and music for the hymn "I Sing the Mighty Power of God" by Isaac Watts. Read and talk about the verses with them. Sing the hymn together.

God Is Sovereign

Have you ever made something using Legos? Do the plastic pieces get to decide how you will put them together? Who decides? Or suppose your dad buys a new lawn mower. Who owns it and gets to decide when, where, and how it will be used? Does your neighbor decide, or does your dad? Now think about the Maker and Creator of all things. Since God created everything, who owns everything?

> The earth is the LORD's and the fullness thereof,
>   the world and those who dwell therein. (Psalm 24:1)

Every single thing in the world belongs to God, including every person. So who has the right to decide how everything will look, how it will act, and what will happen to it? Who gets the final say in whether you have dark hair or light hair? Whether you grow up to be tall or short? Whether or not you will go to the zoo next week? Whether tomorrow will be sunny or cloudy? Whether the farm crops will grow or not grow this year?

> Our God is in the heavens;
>   he does all that he pleases. (Psalm 115:3)

> He does according to his will among the host of heaven
>   and among the inhabitants of the earth;
> and none can stay his hand
>   or say to him, "What have you done?" (Daniel 4:35)

What do these verses mean? They are telling us that God is "sovereign." You have already learned that God is the Creator and is wise and almighty. So, think of God's being "sovereign" as adding these three things together:

God has the RIGHT to do with His creation whatever He decides to do.

God has the WISDOM to make all His plans work out perfectly.

God has the POWER to make all His plans happen. (No one can stop Him. That's what "none can stay his hand" means.)

God is SOVEREIGN—He has the right, wisdom, and power to do as He pleases. In other words, God is in charge. He has the final say. Everything and everyone are under God's authority and rule. God decides when the sun will come up in the morning and when it will go down at night. God controls how many times your heart will beat in a day. God determines how many brothers or sisters you will have. It goes on and on and on.

God is sovereign over everything that happens, every moment of every day.

> "My counsel shall stand,
> and I will accomplish all
> my purpose,"
> calling a bird of prey from
> the east,
> the man of my counsel
> from a far country.
> I have spoken, and I will
> bring it to pass;
> I have purposed, and I will
> do it. (Isaiah 46:10–11)

God's "counsel" is His word, His plans. God's sovereign control over every-thing—even over birds and man—accomplishes everything just as He plans.

In the last chapter, we saw the sovereign God at work. In what ways?

- God was sovereign in choosing Israel to be His specially chosen people.
- God was sovereign over the terrible plagues he sent upon the Egyptians.
- God was sovereign over Pharaoh. After the tenth plague, Pharaoh told Moses,

Up, go out from among my people, both you and the people of Israel; and go, serve the LORD. (Exodus 12:31).

The king's heart is a stream of water in the hand of the LORD;
    he turns it wherever he will. (Proverbs 21:1)

But God's sovereign work didn't stop there. As you know, there is more to this story. As you read the next verses, look carefully for the many different things God sovereignly controlled.

And the LORD hardened the heart of Pharaoh king of Egypt, and he pursued the people of Israel. (Exodus 14:8)

And Moses said to the people, "Fear not, stand firm, and see the salvation of the LORD, which he will work for you today." (Exodus 14:13)

Then Moses stretched out his hand over the sea, and the LORD drove the sea back by a strong east wind all night and made the sea dry land, and the waters were divided. And the people of Israel went into the midst of the sea on dry ground. (Exodus 14:21–22)

Finally, when Israel was safely on the other side of the sea, God had Moses stretch out his hand again, and God returned the waters, destroying all the Egyptian armies. God was sovereign over every detail in this story—over a king's heart, Pharaoh's armies, a huge sea, and more. God saved His people and did it His way in His timing. God had the right, wisdom, and power to do exactly as He pleased.

How did Israel respond to God? How should we act toward a God who is sovereign over all things?

> Israel saw the great power that the LORD used against the Egyptians, so the people feared the LORD, and they believed in the LORD. (Exodus 14:31)

LEARNING TO TRUST GOD

✤ Suppose you were put in charge of flying an airplane for a day. Why would that be a bad thing for you and others? Why is it right and good that God is sovereign over all things? Why can He be trusted to always do what is best? Do you trust Him in every situation? Read and talk about Romans 8:28.

✤ In this story from Exodus, we see two kinds of people—those who tried to fight against God's sovereign control and those who "feared the LORD, and . . . believed in the LORD." Which response is pleasing to God? Does your heart fight against God or gladly believe in Him? How is this shown in your life?

✤ *Activity:* Across the top of a large piece of paper, write out the words of Psalm 115:3. Underneath the verse, draw a large crown. Decorate it to look as special as possible. Underneath the crown, write "God is sovereign." Put the finished picture somewhere as a reminder to trust God.

God Is Self-Sufficient

How many things have you needed since getting out of bed today? Did you remember things like air to breathe, gravity to hold your body in place, the sun to rise and warm the earth? Why do you need so many things? What does this show you about yourself? It shows that you *depend* on things from "outside" yourself in order to live. What kinds of things?

He himself gives to all mankind life and breath and everything. (Acts 17:25)

God is the one who gives us *everything* that we need. All creation depends on God and cannot exist for even one moment apart from Him. God provides us with air, gravity, sunshine, water, food, clothing, houses, families, and everything else. You are like an empty cup. Every day, over and over again, you need to be filled in order to stay alive. Now think of billions of empty cups (all the people in the world) who need the same thing. What a huge, never-ending job it would be to fill all those cups! Yet that's exactly what God does. He provides for our every need over and over and over again. We *need* God. We are completely dependent on Him!

But what about God? Is God dependent on anything? Does He need something to stay alive? Maybe air to breathe? . . . Remember, God is eternal. That means that God was alive *before* there was any air to breathe, water to drink, food to eat, sun for light and warmth, or anything else. What does this tell you about God?

The God who made the world and everything in it, being Lord of heaven and earth, does not live in temples made by man, nor is he served by human hands, as though he needed anything, since he himself gives to all mankind life and breath and everything. (Acts 17:24–25)

God is the Creator of everything. He *does not need* "temples"—houses—made by someone for him to live in. God *does not need* to be served or helped by us in any way. Why? Because God doesn't need anything. God provides us with *everything*, but doesn't need *anything* Himself. That is incredible!

God is SELF-SUFFICIENT—He doesn't need anything.

God alone is self-sufficient. He alone is independent and doesn't need anything outside Himself in order to exist and live—absolutely nothing! That is why God has chosen a very special name for Himself. What is it? In the language in which the Bible was first written, God's very special name was written as "YHWH," which most people pronounce as "Yahweh." But in most Bibles, you will see it written as "Lord" (with capital letters). This name is used more than 6,800 times in the Bible! God's name has a very important meaning. It means "I AM WHO I AM" or "I will be who I will be." In other words, Yahweh is independent and self-sufficient. Yahweh doesn't need anything, nor does He need any help to do great things.

I am the Lord, who made all things,

    who alone stretched out the heavens,

    who spread out the earth by myself. (Isaiah 44:24)

God didn't need help creating the heavens and the earth. He did it all by Himself—with no help from angels and no need to go out to find ingredients or supplies. The self-sufficient God simply spoke with His all-powerful voice, and all things came into being. And God doesn't need help to accomplish His plans—for instance, God didn't need help sending the plagues, defeating Pharaoh, or parting the sea. This is *always and forever* true of God.

Why is it important to know that God is self-sufficient and doesn't need anything? Why is it good news? Here are some questions that hint at the answers.

- What would happen if God needed you to keep the stars in place in the sky?
- What if God needed food from you so He wouldn't grow weak and die?
- What might happen in the world if God needed to take a nap?
- What if God needed your help to solve a hard problem?
- What would it be like if God got sick and needed you to take care of Him?
- What would happen if someone could say to God, "Because You had to borrow money from me, now You have to do what I say"?
- What if you asked God for something, but He said, "I'm sorry—I've run out of that"?

Because God is self-sufficient, we do not need to imagine or worry about any of these situations. The Lord does not need—and will never need—food or sleep or help to hold the stars in place. He does not need anyone to take care of Him. He will never be forced to do what someone else says, nor will He ever run out of anything. God will always be able to provide His people with everything we need. So how should you act toward God?

> Know that the Lord, he is God!
>> It is he who made us, and we are his;
>> we are his people, and the sheep of his pasture.
>
> Enter his gates with thanksgiving,
>> and his courts with praise!
>> Give thanks to him; bless his name! (Psalm 100:3–4)

LEARNING TO TRUST GOD

✦ God doesn't need anything, including people. So why did God create us? For the same reason He created everything: for His glory—to show His greatness and worth! He wants to share the wonders of His greatness with us so that we can enjoy Him most of all. Read Psalm 16:11 and 1 Peter 2:9.

✦ Read and talk about Psalm 121. The words of this psalm are for God's people—everyone who is trusting in Jesus. Could God be depended on to keep these promises if He were not self-sufficient? Why not? Do you look to God to be your helper and keeper? In what ways?

✦ *Activity:* Gather two clear glass jars. On one jar, tape a sign that reads "God is self-sufficient." On the other jar, tape a sign that reads "We need . . ." Place the two jars side by side on your dinner table. Next, have all the members of your family write down or draw pictures of at least five things they need. Place these slips of paper in the "We need . . ." jar. Do this for several days. Before you eat your meals, praise God for being self-sufficient and give thanks for His provision.

God Is Faithful

Have you ever made a promise to someone? Maybe you told your mom, "I promise to clean my room before going to the park." When you make a promise, you are saying, "I will do what I said I would do." Why is it important to keep a promise? We know there are times when people don't keep promises they make. Sometimes they simply forget. Or something happens so they aren't able to keep a promise—maybe they get sick or hurt. And sometimes people lie and make promises they don't plan to keep.

What about God? What kinds of promises does He make? Does He *always* keep His promises? Let's look at some promises He made in the Bible.

- God promised to send a flood to destroy the world because of the wickedness of man. Did God keep His promise? Yes. But God also promised that He would save Noah and his family. Did God keep His promise? Yes. God saved them in the ark (Genesis 6–7).
- God promised that Abraham and Sarah would have a child in their old age. Did God keep His promise? Yes. Sarah gave birth to Isaac (Genesis 17; 21).
- God promised to free Israel from captivity in Egypt. Did God keep His promise? Yes (Exodus 3; 14).
- God promised Joshua that He would give the Israelites a mighty victory over the city of Jericho. Did God keep His promise? Yes. God brought down the walls of Jericho (Joshua 6).

The Bible is filled with thousands of examples of God making and keeping His promises, over and over and over again. Many years after God brought down the walls of Jericho, Joshua (whom God chose to lead Israel after Moses died) said this to the people of Israel:

You know in your hearts and souls, all of you, that not one word has failed of all the good things that the LORD your God promised concerning you. All have come to pass for you; not one of them has failed. (Joshua 23:14)

How many promises did God keep? Every single one! God never forgets or is unable to keep a promise. God never lies about a promise.
God is FAITHFUL—He always does what He says He will do.

Know therefore that the LORD your God is God, the *faithful* God. (Deuteronomy 7:9)

There is a promise that God made before all these other promises:

And the LORD God commanded the man, saying, "You may surely eat of every tree of the garden, but of the tree of the knowledge of good and evil you shall not eat, for in the day that you eat of it you shall surely die." (Genesis 2:16–17)

This promise—"you shall surely die" if you eat from that one tree—was made to Adam in the garden of Eden. God had created Adam and his wife, Eve, to enjoy a very special relationship with God. They were to honor, love, and worship God—obeying Him always and trusting His word. As we know, Adam and Eve disobeyed

God and ate from that one tree. Because of their sin, death entered the world just as God had promised and with it came great sadness and pain. Everything changed after that day.

Adam and Eve were helpless to solve this problem. This was not a surprise to the sovereign God. So, after Adam and Eve sinned, God made a very different kind of promise. God promised that one of Eve's "offspring" (a descendant) would come into the world to save sinners and defeat death—a Savior would come! (See Genesis 3:15.)

So year after year after year, God's sinful people waited for God to keep His promise . . . but no Savior came. Hundreds and hundreds of years passed, but still no Savior came. Had God forgotten His promise? Was God having some kind of trouble keeping it?

God is faithful. So during his people's hundreds of years of waiting, God gave them hints about the promised Savior.

Therefore the Lord himself will give you a sign. Behold, the virgin shall conceive and bear a son, and shall call his name Immanuel. (Isaiah 7:14)

But you, O Bethlehem . . .

. . . .
from you shall come forth for me
    one who is to be ruler in Israel,
whose coming forth is from of old,
    from ancient days. (Micah 5:2)

The Savior would be a baby born in the city of Bethlehem. But . . . one hundred, two hundred, and three hundred years went by and no Savior was born in Bethlehem. Then another one hundred, two hundred, and three hundred years went by—and still no Savior. What was taking so long?

God is both wise and faithful. So at just the right time,

an angel of the Lord appeared to him in a dream, saying, "Joseph, son of David, do not fear to take Mary as your wife, for that which is conceived in her is from the Holy Spirit. She will bear a son, and you shall call his name Jesus, for he will save his people from their sins." (Matthew 1:20–21)

Everything happened just as God promised. God is faithful—He always does what He says He will do!

> O Lord, you are my God;
>   I will exalt you; I will praise your name,
> for you have done wonderful things,
>   plans formed of old, faithful and sure. (Isaiah 25:1)

LEARNING TO TRUST GOD

✦ Can you recall other promises from the Bible? When you see that God always keeps His promises, over and over again, what should that cause you to think, feel, and do? Read and talk about some of God's promises, such as the ones in Psalm 1:6; Isaiah 41:13; Romans 10:9; Philippians 4:19; Hebrews 13:5; 1 John 1:9; 2:25.

✦ Read and talk about Romans 3:23 and 5:12. Why do you need a Savior? Why was Jesus the best promise of all? What did He do to save sinners? What does He promise for all who believe in Him? Read Romans 6:23.

✦ *Activity:* Have your parents help you to find the words and music for the hymn "Every Promise of Your Word" by Keith Getty and Stuart Townend. Read and talk about the verses. Sing the hymn together.

God Is a Trinity

Have you ever looked at pictures of yourself as a baby? What were you like back then? In the last chapter, we learned about the birth of baby Jesus. Do you think that Jesus looked and acted like an ordinary baby? Yes, He was born fully human—with a tiny, weak, and helpless body. Yet the Bible tells us that Jesus is the Savior God had promised. So, although Jesus was ordinary in many ways, He was also *extraordinary*—He was different from any other baby ever born. Before Jesus was born, an angel told Mary,

> The child to be born will be called holy—the Son of God. (Luke 1:35)

Mary was told that Jesus is "the Son of God." So the one eternal God is Jesus's true Father. And just as human sons are like their fathers in many ways, Jesus is like His Father too.

> [Jesus] is the image of the invisible God. (Colossians 1:15)

Pretend you are looking in a mirror. What do you see? An image or picture of yourself. Jesus is a "picture" of His Father—He shows us what God the Father is really like. Jesus is so much like His Father that

> [Jesus] is the radiance of the glory of God and the exact imprint of his nature. (Hebrews 1:3)

> In [Jesus] all the fullness of God was pleased to dwell. (Colossians 1:19)

Imagine for a moment that you wrote out on a piece of paper all the things that are true about God the Father—for instance, that He is Eternal, Glorious,

Wise, Almighty, Sovereign, Self-Sufficient, Faithful. . . . What would happen if you made an *exact* copy of your list? What would it look like? It would look *exactly* like the first paper and have all the same words. This copy, which would share the exact same list as your first paper, can help you to better understand that Jesus, God's Son, shares His Father's *exact and full* nature. Everything that is true of the Father is true of His Son. How can this be?

> In the beginning was the Word [Jesus], and the Word was with God, and the Word was God. . . . And the Word became flesh and dwelt among us. (John 1:1, 14)

Why is Jesus, the Son of God, so much like His Father? Because Jesus *is* fully and truly God. When Jesus came to earth as a baby, He also became fully and truly human! So the one true God is "God the Father" and "God the Son." But there is something else that you must know and understand about who God is and what He is like. There is Someone we haven't mentioned yet. Who is that?

> [Jesus said,] "Go therefore and make disciples of all nations, baptizing them in the name of the Father and of the Son and of the Holy Spirit." (Matthew 28:19)

Who is the missing "Person" mentioned in this verse? The Holy Spirit. The Holy Spirit is also fully and truly God. Therefore, just as God the Father and God the Son are eternal, almighty, faithful . . . so is the Holy Spirit.

So, who is God? God is three "persons," and each is truly and fully God: God the Father, God the Son, and God the Holy Spirit. That's a little strange, isn't it? Does that mean that there are three separate Gods? Isn't there only one true God? Yes, there is only one true God (Deuteronomy 6:4).

How can there be three persons, each fully and truly God, but only one God? It is probably one of the most mysterious things about God. It will always be more than we can fully understand. But it is the *truth*. There is a special word used to describe this special quality about God. **God is a TRINITY—God is three persons in one God: Father, Son, and Holy Spirit.**

Why is it important to know that God is a Trinity? Because it is only through knowing, loving, trusting, and worshiping this one true God that we can be saved. Each person of the Trinity is necessary for our joy in God. Here are two reasons why:

> [God the Father] has delivered us from the domain of darkness and transferred us to the kingdom of his beloved Son, in whom we have redemption, the forgiveness of sins. (Colossians 1:13–14)

[Jesus said,] "But the Helper, the Holy Spirit, whom the Father will send in my name, he will teach you all things and bring to your remembrance all that I have said to you." (John 14:26)

Here is one last question: How should you respond to this mysterious truth about God?

Let us offer to God acceptable worship, with reverence and awe. (Hebrews 12:28)

LEARNING TO TRUST GOD

✦ When you read the Bible, do you keep the Trinity in mind? Do you look to see the work of the Father, Son, and Holy Spirit? Why is it so important to know and believe the truth of the Trinity? Can a person worship God without recognizing who He really, truly is? Why not?

✦ Because Jesus became fully human, did people sometimes treat Him as if He were just a man? Can you think of times when Jesus showed people His "God-ness"? Read and talk about Colossians 1:16–20. Why is trusting in Jesus the only way to have a right relationship with the triune God?

✦ *Activity:* Gather four identical envelopes. Write the following four phrases— one on each envelope: *There is only one God*; *God the Father*; *God the Son*; *God the Holy Spirit.* Fold the last three envelopes in half and place them into the "There is only one God" envelope. One by one, take out the three envelopes and recite *God the Father is God; God the Son is God; God the Holy Spirit is God.* Then place each back inside the "There is only one God" envelope and recite *There is only one God.* Show this to a sibling or friend.

God Is Happy

What is one of your favorite things to do in the whole world? Why do you enjoy doing it?

Do you always get to do your favorite thing? For example, suppose you really like playing baseball. Is there anything that might stop you from playing? Yes. How does that make you feel? Or can doing your favorite thing get a little boring after a while? Yes, it can. (Imagine eating your favorite ice cream . . . and nothing else, day after day.)

Did you know that God—Father, Son, and Holy Spirit (the Trinity)—has a favorite thing He enjoys doing all the time? Something that nothing can stop Him from doing? Something that He never, ever gets bored of doing? What could it be? God's favorite thing is . . . being God! Think about this for a moment: God alone is eternal and has existed before anything else. The three persons of the Trinity have always enjoyed perfect fellowship with one another. God is perfect in every way: in his wisdom, might, sovereignty, self-sufficiency, and more. Nothing about being God ever grows boring. Nothing and no one can stop God from being God and doing exactly what He wants to do. That is why the Bible says that

> [God] is the blessed and only Sovereign, the King of kings and Lord of lords. (1 Timothy 6:15)

Who alone has the right, wisdom, and power to do all that He pleases? Who rules over all? The "blessed" God. The word "blessed" means "happy."

God is HAPPY—He delights in being God.

Why is it important to know that God is a happy God? Well, think about a time when you were super happy about something. Did you show it in a certain way? Did your happiness spill over into a big smile, laughing, jumping up and down, cheering, or clapping? Could others see and hear your happiness? God's happiness in being God is millions of times greater. It's so great that it spills over too. What does this look like?

> O Lord, how manifold are your works!
>> In wisdom have you made them all;
>> the earth is full of your creatures.
> Here is the sea, great and wide,
>> which teems with creatures innumerable,
>> living things both small and great.
> There go the ships,
>> and Leviathan,[1] which you formed to play in it. (Psalm 104:24–26)

Did God create the world in just black, white, and gray? (Think how boring that would be!) No. God created the world in all sorts of beautiful colors, interesting shapes, and different sizes. Just think of the "innumerable" (too many to count) creatures that live in the sea—things like clown fish, seahorses, octopuses, starfish, jellyfish, sea urchins, shrimp, eels, stingrays, seals, otters, sharks, and so many more. And then there are the giant whales and dolphins that jump and splash and play. These amazing creatures, in all their shapes, sizes, and colors, show the happiness of their Creator!

1. Possibly referring to sea "monsters"—large creatures such as whales and dolphins.

> May the glory of the LORD endure forever;
>> may the LORD rejoice in his works. (Psalm 104:31)

God's happiness doesn't just spill over into His creation. God's happiness can also be seen in what He does for His people.

> The LORD your God is in your midst,
>> a mighty one who will save;
> he will rejoice over you with gladness;
>> he will quiet you by his love;
> he will exult over you with loud singing. (Zephaniah 3:17)

What does the Lord God do for His people? He saves them! What is His attitude in doing this? Is He grumpy about it, saying, "Oh, I guess I had better save them. What a bother"? No, not at all! God is happy to do it! He rejoices over His people with gladness. God is so happy that He even sings loudly over His people. Yes, the happy God sings!

Why is God's happiness important for you? Why does it matter? Because God made each of us with a very strong desire to be happy. We are always looking for things to make us happy—foods, activities, friends, hobbies, and more. But none of these things can make us happy forever. They will all get boring, break apart, move away, or disappoint us in some way. God wants you to be happy, and He knows that there is one way for you to *always and forever* be happy.

> You make known to me the path of life;
>> in your presence there is fullness of joy;
>> at your right hand are pleasures forevermore. (Psalm 16:11)

God is happy to show you that He alone can give you "fullness of joy"—complete happiness. Being in God's presence means enjoying "pleasures"—wonderful, exciting, and good things—forever! God is not like a grumpy old man. He is never boring. He will never stop being a happy God. His people will be able to enjoy His happiness all the time. But what is the "path of life" to enjoying the happiness of God always and forever?

[Jesus said,] "I am the way, and the truth, and the life." (John 14:6)

LEARNING TO TRUST GOD

✦ Have you ever thought about God being the happiest person in the universe? Suppose God was sovereign but not happy. Why would that be bad news? Why is it good news that God is happy and that He always delights in being God? Are you depending on God to make you happy? How does your life show this? Who is the "path" to enjoying "fullness of joy"?

✦ God is always happy being God. But we also learn in the Bible that there are things that sadden and even anger God. (For example, a man can enjoy being a daddy and yet be rightly saddened and angered by his child's disobedience.) Can you give some examples from the Bible? Even when God is rightly saddened and angered by man's sin, He is never frustrated. He is still the "blessed and only Sovereign." God still delights in being God and is working out His perfect plans exactly as He pleases.

✦ *Activity:* With your parents' help, find pictures of all kinds of sea creatures. Learn about several of them. How do they show the happiness of God? Read and talk about Psalm 92:4.

God Is Love

Pretend for a minute that you fell and scraped your knee really badly. You cried out to your mom for help, and she said, "Go get yourself a bandage" and then went back to her work. Or suppose you had a bad nightmare and cried out in the dark to your dad, and he said, "Turn on your light and leave me alone." Would you be happy with either of those responses? What else would you want and need? Maybe some extra attention, comfort, a hug, and reassuring words? Yes, those are ways of showing love. Love involves treasuring someone so much that you want to give them whatever would make them joyful.

Do you know that God treasures someone too? Who could it be?

> The LORD your God has chosen you to be a people for his treasured possession, out of all the peoples who are on the face of the earth. (Deuteronomy 7:6)

God treasures His specially chosen people! Now think about this: If your own parents show their love for you in special ways, can you imagine how much better and greater God's love is for His specially chosen people? What does God give to His people? Well, as we learned in another chapter, God gives *all* people "life and breath and everything" (Acts 17:25). But His *own* people need much more than that to be truly happy.

> He will tend his flock like a shepherd;
> he will gather the lambs in his arms. (Isaiah 40:11)

> I will strengthen you, I will help you,
> I will uphold you with my righteous right hand. (Isaiah 41:10)

For the Lord has comforted his people

   and will have compassion on his afflicted. (Isaiah 49:13)

He has said, "I will *never* leave you nor *forsake* you." (Hebrews 13:5)

All these verses, and many more, show God's special love for His people. God doesn't just provide us with air, water, food, and a place to live. God also gives His people things like comfort, care, compassion, reassurance, help, and courage. That is loving. God's love is a love that never will run out because it comes from the eternal, self-sufficient God. It is a love that will always and forever give God's people "fullness of joy" because it comes from a happy God. It is a love that can never be broken or grow weak because it comes from a faithful and almighty God. In fact, all true love comes from God because

God is love. (1 John 4:16)

God is LOVE—He gives of Himself for the joy of others.

Just how great is the love of God? How much has God given of Himself for our joy?

> For God so loved the world, that he gave his only Son. (John 3:16)

The most loving thing that God has ever done for us has been to give us His Son. First of all, God sent Jesus into the world as a human baby. Jesus took on the role of a humble servant and lived among His people. While Jesus lived on earth, He healed the sick, blind, lame, and dying. He spent time with His disciples and others. He taught crowds and miraculously fed them when they grew hungry. Jesus gave His attention to outcasts—people no one else wanted to be around. These are all examples of how Jesus gave of Himself for the joy of others. But there is more—much, much more—to God's love.

> But God shows his love for us in that while we were still sinners, Christ died for us. (Romans 5:8)

God the Father gave to the world His *greatest* treasure—Someone He loves most of all: His own Son. The most loving thing God has done has been to "give up" His Son—to put Jesus to death on the cross—in order to save sinful people. Jesus loves sinners just as His Father does, and He gave up His life willingly. How does this bring God's people joy?

> For God so loved the world, that he gave his only Son, that whoever believes in him should not perish but have eternal life. (John 3:16)

God the Father gave up His greatest treasure so that we might be able to have lasting joy with Him forever. This promise of eternal life is for all of God's specially chosen people. Who are they? Everyone who believes in Jesus, who trusts in Him as their one and only Savior.

Here is an amazing, wonderful, better-than-you-could-ever-imagine description of God's love for His people:

He who did not spare his own Son but gave him up for us all, how will he not also with him graciously give us all things? . . . I am sure that neither death nor life, nor angels nor rulers, nor things present nor things to come, nor powers, nor height nor depth, nor anything else in all creation, will be able to separate us from the love of God in Christ Jesus our Lord. (Romans 8:32, 38–39)

LEARNING TO TRUST GOD

+ Read Romans 5:8 and John 3:16 again. Why is this the most loving thing God could do for you? In what ways has He shown you His amazing love? What is the right way to respond to His love?

+ When someone gives you something that brings you great joy, what do you want to do with it? Keep it to yourself, or share it with others? Why? If you have received God's love, what does He want you to do? What did Jesus's disciples do? How could you share the love of Jesus with one other person this week?

+ *Activity:* Make a thank-you card to God. Fold a stiff piece of paper in half to form a card. On the top of the outside of the card, write "God is LOVE—He gives of Himself for the joy of others." Underneath this, draw a picture of a cross. Cut out a heart shape and glue it onto the center of the cross. Open the card and write a note thanking God for loving you and giving up His Son to die for the sins of His people. Place the card somewhere where it will be a daily reminder.

God Is Omnipresent

Have you ever wanted to be in two different places at the same time? Maybe a friend invited you over to play and, at the same time, your parents promised to take you to the park. You want to do both! But of course you can't be in two places at once. None of us can. We have physical bodies that limit us to being in one place at a time.

But what about God? Can He only be in one place at a time? See if you can find the answer in these verses written by King David.

> Where shall I go from your Spirit?
>   Or where shall I flee from your presence?
> If I ascend to heaven, you are there!
>   If I make my bed in Sheol, you are there!
> If I take the wings of the morning
>   and dwell in the uttermost parts of the sea,
> even there your hand shall lead me,
>   and your right hand shall hold me. (Psalm 139:7–10)

David wondered, "Is there anywhere that I could go where God wouldn't be?" What was the answer? No matter where David might go—up in the heavens, down deep in the ground, or far across the sea—God would be there. Is that because God would simply follow David around?

> Do I not fill heaven and earth? declares the Lord. (Jeremiah 23:24)

> But will God indeed dwell on the earth? Behold, heaven and the highest heaven cannot contain you. (1 Kings 8:27)

These verses tell us that God is not limited by a physical body like we are. God is spirit and is everywhere all the time. God is not "contained" or limited by space. Here is an illustration that might help: Suppose your mom is baking a pizza in the oven. Does the wonderful smell from the pizza just stay in the oven? No, it fills the house. This example can help you to better understand that God is not contained or limited by space. He "fills" heaven and earth. There is a word that describes this important truth about God.

God is OMNIPRESENT—He is everywhere all the time. "Omni" means "all." God is "all-present."

Why is this good news for God's people? In the last chapter, we learned that God is love. We also learned that God especially loves His chosen people—everyone who is trusting in Jesus. One of the ways that God loves His people is by *always* being with them (Isaiah 41:10; Hebrews 13:5). That means God will *always be with* Elizabeth in the United States, Juan in Mexico, Herbert in Kenya, Sarah in Jordan, Suresh in India, Adrian in Russia, Ronan in Ireland, Michelle in Australia—He will be with His people all over the world, all the time, every hour of every day.

The omnipresent God never needs to leave you in order to be with someone else. You are never truly alone, even at night. God is always watching over His people.

But not everyone wants God to be "present" all the time. Some people want to try to hide from God. In the Old Testament, Jonah tried that. Why? Because God told him to go to the great city of Nineveh and "call out against it, for their evil" (Jonah 1:2). Jonah didn't like God's plan, so instead of going to Nineveh, he hopped on a ship traveling in the opposite direction. Jonah wanted to "flee . . . from the presence of the LORD" (Jonah 1:3). Well, the omnipresent God was there, and He sent a mighty storm on the sea. The other men on the ship blamed Jonah and threw him into the sea. But guess who was there? God! He sent a large fish to swallow Jonah. So, there was Jonah in the dark, slimy belly of a fish. Finally, Jonah called out to God, who was *there* and heard his prayer! Jonah had learned an important lesson.

> Can a man hide himself in secret places so that I cannot see him? declares the LORD. Do I not fill heaven and earth? declares the LORD. (Jeremiah 23:24)

Why should this matter to you? Because you, like Jonah, cannot hide from God. Suppose you steal a cookie before dinner, thinking, *Mom won't see me.* God is there, and He sees what is happening.

So, how should you act toward the omnipresent God? Should you ignore Him and pretend He isn't there watching over you? Should you try to run away and hide from Him? What would be the *opposite* of ignoring God? What would be the *opposite* of trying to hide from Him? Here is what Jonah did:

> Then Jonah prayed to the LORD his God from the belly of the fish, saying,
>
> "I called out to the LORD, out of my distress,
>   and he answered me.
>
> . . . .

When my life was fainting away,
   I remembered the LORD,
and my prayer came to you,
   into your holy temple." (Jonah 2:1–2, 7)

Seek the LORD and his strength;
   Seek his presence continually! (1 Chronicles 16:11)

LEARNING TO TRUST GOD

✢ Before Jesus returned to heaven after His resurrection, He made special promises to His disciples. Read Matthew 28:20 and then John 14:16–17. Have you been helped by these promises? How? What steps could you take this week to seek the Lord?

✢ Have you ever tried to be like Jonah and run from God? Do you try to go about your life as if God isn't really there (ignoring Him)? How do Jonah's actions warn you about doing this? How does Jonah's prayer from the belly of the fish serve as an example of what you should do? Who do you need to seek after and call out to? Read Romans 10:13 and 1 John 1:9.

✢ *Activity:* Write out Jeremiah 23:24 on a large piece of stiff paper. Next, cut the paper into five to ten pieces. Have another person hide the pieces throughout your house. See how quickly you can find the pieces and put them together correctly. Play the game with your siblings too, taking turns hiding and finding the pieces.

God Is Unchanging

Do you have photos of yourself taken at different ages? Maybe even a photo album that shows you as a tiny baby, followed by page after page of new photos added as you grew older? Do you look the same now as you did two years ago? Four years ago? What kinds of changes have you experienced since you were a baby? Can you imagine what you might be like fifty years from now?

We all change over time. Some of those changes are good. For example, as you grow older and exercise and eat healthy foods, you will become bigger and stronger. As you spend time learning new things, you will become smarter. But some changes we experience are very different. Your body may get sick, or you might hurt your arm while playing. An older person may start to lose his hearing or become forgetful. But it's not just people who experience changes—all creation changes.

> Of old you laid the foundation of the earth,
>   and the heavens are the work of your hands.
> They will perish, but you will remain;
>   they will all wear out like a garment.
> You will change them like a robe, and they will pass away,
>   but you are the same, and your years have no end. (Psalm 102:25–27)

Even the foundation of the earth—like a huge, hard rock—changes over time and wears away. Big rocks get broken down by wind and waves and become tiny pieces of soft sand. The seasons change, and trees lose their leaves. Beautiful flowers bloom and then fade, wither away, and die. They all wear out like a "garment" (clothing). After all, what happens to your play clothes over time? But these verses tell us something very important about God. He is different from these things in a very special way: "You [God] are the same, and your years have no end." What does it mean that God will be "the same" forever?

Pretend for a minute that you have a photo album showing who God is and what He is like from year to year. What might you see as you turn the pages? Each page of this pretend photo album would look exactly the same as the one before it. From everlasting to everlasting, God remains the same, never changing in any

way. For example, from everlasting God has been almighty. He is all-powerful. He didn't need to grow up, eat right, and exercise in order to become almighty. He has always been almighty. And God will never become weaker with old age—He will remain almighty to everlasting.

> For I the LORD do not change. (Malachi 3:6)

Unlike everything else in creation, **God is UNCHANGING—He never changes.** He cannot change and become better because He is already perfect in every way—He is the best. God does not change, so He will *always* remain perfect in every way. Why is this important to know? Let's look at one reason:

> The name of the LORD is a strong tower;
>   the righteous man runs into it and is safe. (Proverbs 18:10)

This verse describes God as being like a strong tower for His people. When you run to God by trusting in Jesus, God will keep you safe forever. Now imagine for a moment what would happen if God were *not* unchanging. Suppose over time God got old and weak and was no longer almighty. He would be like an old crumbling tower that is no longer a place of safety. Or what if God became old and forgetful? What if He changed from being faithful to all His promises to forgetting His promises?

For example, Jesus promised,

> I am the door. If anyone enters by me, he will be saved. (John 10:9)

But what if Jesus changed His mind and didn't want to keep this promise anymore? Because God is unchanging, something like that will never, ever happen. God can be depended upon all the time, always and forever.

Jesus Christ [who is God] is the *same* yesterday and today and forever. (Hebrews 13:8)

God is unchanging. He will never change who He is or what He is like. God will never change His mind about His promises or purposes either. You can depend upon Him always and forever.

Trust in him at all times, O people;
    pour out your heart before him;
    God is a refuge for us. (Psalm 62:8)

LEARNING TO TRUST GOD

✢ Talk about some good changes you've recently experienced. Now talk about some bad changes you've experienced, not only in yourself but also in the world around you. Why do some changes feel sad and scary? Why is it good news that God is unchanging?

✢ Review Proverbs 18:10. Do you see God as a strong tower? Why is it good that God never changes His mind about His promises? Why is it good to know that He will not change the way in which we can be saved? (See John 10:9 again.) How can you remind yourself this week that God is unchanging?

✢ *Activity:* With your parents, find the words to the hymn "Immortal, Invisible, God Only Wise" by Walter Chalmers Smith. Print out the words if you can. Carefully read through each verse and see how many attributes of God (words describing who God is and what He is like) you discover. Sing the hymn together.

God Is Omniscient

Have you ever had to take a test for school? What kinds of questions were on the test? What is the purpose of taking a test? Tests are used to measure and determine what you know about something. Now suppose you had these questions on a test: *(1) How much do all the oceans, rivers, and lakes weigh? (2) How much do all the mountains weigh? (3) What is the size of the entire universe?* Would you know the answers? Why not? Is there someone who would know?

> [God] has measured the waters in the hollow of his hand
>> and marked off the heavens with a span,
> enclosed the dust of the earth in a measure
>> and weighed the mountains in scales. (Isaiah 40:12)

God knows exactly how much water there is and what it weighs. God knows how much all the mountains weigh. God knows exactly how big outer space is. He created all these huge things and knows everything about them. But what about tiny things or hidden things? Does God know all about those kinds of things, too?

> For you formed my inward parts;
>> you knitted me together in my mother's womb. (Psalm 139:13)

When your life first began, you were too tiny to be seen. You were hidden inside your mother. But God knew everything about you even then because He was the one making you. He knows all about your bones, muscles, heart—everything about your insides and outsides. He also knows things about you that seem unimportant—like the very number of hairs on your head (Matthew

10:30). That is amazing! But *God knows even more* than how much you weigh, how big you are, what you look like, or how many hairs you have on your head.

> You know when I sit down and when I rise up.
> . . . .
> You search out my path and my lying down
>   and are acquainted with all my ways.
>   (Psalm 139:2–3)

God knows what time you got out of bed this morning, what you ate for breakfast, and what you are doing right now. God knows all your actions and activities, and even the actions and activities of all people every-where in the world, at every moment. But *God knows even more.*

> Even before a word is on my tongue,
>   behold, O Lᴏʀᴅ, you know it altogether.
>   (Psalm 139:4)

God knows every word you will say even before you open your mouth to say it. Imagine how many words come out of the mouth of every person, every single day. That's a lot of words that God knows. But *God knows even more.*

> You discern my thoughts from afar. (Psalm 139:2)

To "discern" means to know. God knows all your thoughts. He knows what each person is thinking, all the time. But *God knows even more.*

He knows the secrets of the heart. (Psalm 44:21)

God knows all your secrets, even the things that you keep hidden from others, deep down in your heart—feelings of sadness or fear or envy. God knows what's deep in the heart of every person! But *God knows even more.*

> In your book were written, every one of them,
>> the days that were formed for me,
>> when as yet there was none of them. (Psalm 139:16)

This verse is telling us that God knows exactly how many days each person will live on this earth. He knows how many birthdays you will celebrate in the future. God has decided just the right number for each person. But *God knows even more* than this.

> I am God, and there is none like me,
> declaring the end from the beginning
>> and from ancient times things not yet done. (Isaiah 46:9–10)

God knows everything about the past—things from "the beginning" and "ancient times"—but He also knows "things not yet done." That means God knows everything that will happen in the future—all our activities, all our choices, and everything else that will happen in the world. God doesn't just make good guesses about what might happen; He knows because He "declares" it, meaning that God has decided exactly what will happen. We don't know what will happen the rest of today, tomorrow, next year, or even ten years from now. But God knows for certain.

So, if someone were to ask you, "How much does God know?" what would be a correct one-word answer? Everything! (See 1 John 3:20.) There is a special word that describes this truth about God.

God is OMNISCIENT—He knows everything. (Remember that "omni" means "all." God is "all-knowing.")

How should you respond to an omniscient God?

Search me, O God, and know my heart!
    Try me and know my thoughts!
And see if there be any grievous way in me,
    and lead me in the way everlasting! (Psalm 139:23–24)

LEARNING TO TRUST GOD

✛ Because God knows everything, where is the best source of answers to the most important questions? For example, who *knows* exactly how the world came into existence? Who *knows* what is true about being a boy or a girl? Why is it important to look to the Bible for answers? Do you trust God's Word to give you true knowledge?

✛ Why is it good that God knows everything about you, even your deepest thoughts and feelings? Are there times when you have felt misunderstood? Does God know? Why is that comforting? Why might it sometimes feel like a bad thing that God knows your heart? Read Psalm 139:23–24 again.

✛ *Activity:* Make flash cards to review the fourteen attributes of God that we have learned about so far. Gather fourteen index cards (or fourteen pieces of paper all cut to the same size). Write an attribute of God on each one. Use the back of the card to write the meaning of the attribute. For example, write "Omniscient" on one side of one of the cards and on the other side write, "God knows everything."

God Is Good

Decide whether the following things are "good" to do: eating an entire bag of candy, helping your mom wash the dishes, watching television all morning, driving the car to a park, doing your schoolwork, arguing with your brother or sister, taking medicine. Would your mom and dad agree with all your answers? How about your siblings?

We aren't the best judges of what is truly good. Sometimes we determine what is "good" by how it makes us feel—by whether or not we enjoy it. For example, you might enjoy eating a bag of candy—"It's so yummy and good!" But that doesn't mean it *is* good for you. Is there anyone who is always able to judge what is truly good? God is. Why does God always know what is truly good? Because

No one is good except God alone. (Mark 10:18)

God alone is truly good. That means everything about God is good—His power, wisdom, faithfulness, sovereign rule, love, and more. Because God alone is truly good, everything that is good comes from Him. God is also the measure of what is truly good.

Here is an illustration that may help to explain this: Suppose you need *exactly* ten inches of string. Would you use your fingers to measure ten inches, or would you use a ruler? Which would provide the right measurement? In a similar way, God provides the right measure for what is truly good. When God judges something to be good, it is truly good. And because God is good, everything He does is good.

You [God] are good and do good. (Psalm 119:68)

The LORD is good to all,
and his mercy is over all that he has made. (Psalm 145:9)

Think of all the thousands upon thousands of good things that God does every single day. God makes the sun shine, bringing us light and warmth. He sends rain to water the plants so that we can enjoy all sorts of delicious foods. He provides us with family and friends. He causes nighttime to come so that our bodies can rest. And notice that the verse said "the LORD is good to all"—"all" includes every person in the world. God is even good to people who don't love and trust Him. Even evil people experience His goodness over and over again.

God is GOOD—He is good in all He is and does.

But God is especially good to His people. Here are some promises He has made to them:

No good thing does he withhold
    from those who walk uprightly. (Psalm 84:11)

Oh, how abundant is your goodness,
    which you have stored up for those who fear you. (Psalm 31:19)

I am the good shepherd. The good shepherd lays down his life for the sheep. (John 10:11)

But is it always easy to see and recognize God's goodness in your life? What if you get hurt? What if someone is mean to you? What if there is not enough to eat? What if a storm damages your house? . . . Is God still good? Is He doing good in these situations? Imagine for a moment that you are very sick, and your parents take you to the doctor. The doctor decides to give you a shot in your arm. Ouch! That will really hurt! Is the doctor being bad? No, the doctor knows that the painful shot is for your good. It is meant to heal your body. This can help you to better understand God's goodness. Just like the doctor, God sometimes brings painful things into your life that later turn out to be good for you.

Do you remember the story of Joseph? What bad things happened to him? He was hated by his brothers and sold as a slave. He was taken far away from his father to the land of Egypt. He was put into prison for a crime he hadn't done. Those are all terrible things! But this is what Joseph said to his brothers when he was finally (by God's wise plan) reunited with them:

As for you, you meant evil against me, but God meant it for good, to bring it about that many people should be kept alive, as they are today. (Genesis 50:20)

God planned all those bad experiences in Joseph's life to bring about His good purposes. God had never stopped being good or doing good. But it is sometimes hard to recognize God's goodness in a situation until we see the final picture—the end—of what God was doing.

And we know that for those who love God all things work together for good, for those who are called according to his purpose. (Romans 8:28)

If you trust in Jesus, God will take even the bad things that happen to you and make them work for your good—every single time without fail. And better yet, God's goodness toward His children will never end.

> Surely goodness and mercy shall follow me
>> all the days of my life,
> and I shall dwell in the house of the LORD
>> forever. (Psalm 23:6)

> Praise the LORD!
> Oh give thanks to the LORD, for he is good,
>> for his steadfast love endures forever! (Psalm 106:1)

LEARNING TO TRUST GOD

✤ Because God is the only perfect judge of what is truly good, where should we go to find out what is truly good? For example, is stealing good or bad? Where would you find the right answer? Read and talk about Psalm 119:68.

✤ How many ways has God been good to you today? Take a minute and see if you can quickly name at least ten ways that He has been good. Has something ever happened in your life that made it hard for you to believe that God is good? What can help you during times like that? What verses and examples can remind you of God's goodness?

✤ *Activity:* Choose one of the verses presented in this chapter to memorize. Write out the verse on a sturdy piece of paper. Decorate the paper to make it look special. Place the verse where you will see it often. Recite the verse throughout the day.

God Is Jealous

Have you ever participated in a contest? Maybe a music competition, spelling challenge, or sporting event? Pretend for a moment that you are participating in a special race. The first-place prize is a beautiful trophy. You line up at the starting line and, as soon as the buzzer sounds, you take off running. You run so fast that you pass by runner after runner until you reach the finish line—you are the winner! But then something incredible happens. When it comes time for you to receive the first-place trophy, one of the other runners grabs it and claims it for himself, saying, "I won. I'm the fastest and best. Cheer for me!" What would you think about that? Should you and the others cheer for him?

The true winner is the one who deserves the first-place trophy. It wouldn't be right for someone else to steal it and demand to be treated as if he had won. It would also be wrong for the crowd to cheer for him. In the Bible, there is a story about someone trying to steal first place from the true winner. Here is what happened . . .

A long time ago, God told the Israelites to build a very special type of box. It looked something like a golden treasure chest and was called the "ark of the covenant." This ark was to remind Israel that the Lord (Yahweh) was the one true God and that He was always present with His people. The people of Israel were to always keep the ark with them and treat it with great respect and care.

But one day, something terrible happened. Israel's enemy, the Philistines, won a battle against Israel and then carried the ark away to a place called Ashdod. They put the ark in the house of Dagon. Dagon was an idol—a false god—that the Philistines worshiped. So the ark of the Lord was now placed next to an idol. Here is what happened next . . .

And when the people of Ashdod rose early the next day, behold, Dagon had fallen face downward on the ground before the ark of the LORD. So they took Dagon and put him back in his place. But when they rose early on the next morning, behold, Dagon had fallen face downward on the ground before the ark of the LORD, and the head of Dagon and both his hands were lying cut off on the threshold. Only the trunk of Dagon was left to him. (1 Samuel 5:3–4)

Why do you think that Dagon kept falling down before the ark of the Lord? Had someone snuck in during the night and pushed Dagon? Hmm . . . it doesn't say that, does it? So, what happened? Well, let's compare Dagon to the Lord God. Was Dagon eternal like God? No, Dagon was made by people using stone or wood. Was Dagon almighty like God? No, Dagon had to be carried by people. Was Dagon unchanging like God? No, Dagon broke apart when he fell. Was Dagon omniscient like God? No, Dagon was a lifeless idol that didn't know anything. And we could go on and on. Idols like Dagon cannot compare with the one true God. So, if this had been a type of contest for who was the great-est and best, who would have won first place every time? Who would deserve all the cheers, applause, and praise?

I am the LORD; that is my
    name;
  my glory I give to no other,
  nor my praise to carved
    idols. (Isaiah 42:8)

The Lord God will not share first place. That is why He caused Dagon to keep falling down. God will never say something like "Even though I'm the best and I'm the true winner, it's okay for someone else to steal first place from Me." God would not be right to share His glory—His greatness and worth—with anything or anyone else. Nor will He share the honor and praise He so rightly deserves.

> For you shall worship no other god, for the LORD, whose name is Jealous, is a jealous God. (Exodus 34:14)

God is "jealous." These words were written after the people of Israel had made an idol to worship. They made a golden calf while Moses was up on Mount Sinai receiving the tablets of the Ten Commandments from God. What happened to that golden calf and the people who worshiped it? Moses

> took the calf that they had made and burned it with fire and ground it to powder and scattered it on the water and made the people of Israel drink it. (Exodus 32:20)

And even worse things happened after that! God is very serious about protecting and guarding His first-place position.

God is JEALOUS—He will not share His glory or the honor and praise He deserves.

Why should it matter to you that God is jealous? After all, you probably don't have an idol like Dagon or a golden calf that you worship. But . . . does something else ever have first place in your heart, something that you treat as more important than God? Maybe toys, computer games, family, friends, television, pets, sports, or music? Do you ever put yourself in first place by wanting to be the center of attention or wanting things your way? All those things can become like idols. Will God share first place with those things? Because God is jealous, it will never be okay for us to treat other things or people as if they are more important than God. He will always be the greatest and best!

> Praise the LORD!
> Praise God in his sanctuary;
>> praise him in his mighty heavens!
> Praise him for his mighty deeds;
>> praise him according to his excellent greatness! (Psalm 150:1–2)

> For great is the LORD, and greatly to be praised;
>> he is to be feared above all gods. (Psalm 96:4)

LEARNING TO TRUST GOD

✦ Imagine how wrong it would feel to have a first-place trophy stolen from you. If you can feel the wrongness of this, imagine how much worse it is when others try to rob God of the praise and honor that He so rightly deserves! Are there things in your own life that you put in first place instead of God? Is God okay with this? What do you need to do? What will help to remind you that God deserves the highest honor and praise?

✦ Think of your favorite cereal for a moment. Suppose someone came along and replaced the cereal inside the box with garbage. Would this be a good substitute? Why not? Why is it a good thing that God is jealous for His greatness and worth? Why is it good that He won't allow substitutes? (Hint: Read Psalm 16:11.)

✦ *Activity:* Use a large piece of paper to cut out the shape of a trophy. Write "God is Jealous" across the top. Below this, write the attributes of God that you have learned so far. Decorate the trophy to make it look very special.

God Is Righteous

Suppose a friend wants to show you a special treasure. You race over to her house to see it. When you get there, she's hugging a bucket of stinky, disgusting garbage and saying, "Isn't my treasure wonderful? It must be worth a fortune. I absolutely *love* it!" Hmm . . . is your friend right to say that stinky garbage is valuable? Is she right to love it? Who should decide what's right? Your friend? You?

> I the LORD speak the truth;
> > I declare what is right. (Isaiah 45:19)

God is the one who determines what is right. So, when God says, "I am the Lord, who made all things" (Isaiah 44:24), that is right. When He says, "I am God, and there is no other" (Isaiah 46:9), that is right. The Bible uses a special word to show that God is always right.

> Righteous are you, O LORD. (Psalm 119:137)

> The LORD is righteous in all his ways. (Psalm 145:17)

God is RIGHTEOUS—everything He thinks, says, and does is right.

So, when God created some animals to be colorful and others to be drab, that was right. God was right in choosing Israel to be His chosen people. God was right in sending His Son into the world as a human baby. God is also right in the way He judges people and decides whether they have done the right thing or the wrong thing. For example, when God flooded the world because of man's wickedness, that was a right and fair judgment.

He judges the world with righteousness;

    he judges the peoples with uprightness. (Psalm 9:8)

But how are people to know what is right and wrong? Do we have to just guess? No. Here is what the Bible says:

The rules of the LORD are true,

    and righteous altogether. (Psalm 19:9)

So the law is holy, and the commandment is holy and righteous and good. (Romans 7:12)

From beginning to end, the Bible is filled with these righteous rules and commands for us to follow and obey. They tell us what is right and wrong. Here are some commands found in Scripture:

- "You shall have no other gods before me."
- "Honor your father and mother."
- "You shall not steal."
- "You shall not bear false witness against your neighbor."
- "You shall love the LORD your God with all your heart and with all your soul and with all your might."

One of the very important jobs Jesus came to do while He lived on earth was to follow and obey all of God's righteous commands. Do you think that would be easy or hard to do? How about when Satan, the devil, was trying really hard to get Jesus to do the wrong thing? Did Jesus obey God then? Here is what happened:

> [Jesus] was led by the Spirit in the wilderness for forty days, being tempted by the devil. And he ate nothing during those days. And when they were ended, he was hungry. The devil said to him, "If you are the Son of God, command this stone to become bread." And Jesus answered him, "It is written, 'Man shall not live by bread alone.'" (Luke 4:1–4)

Yes, Jesus is God and could have turned stones into bread. But Jesus knew that the devil was trying to get Him to get food in the wrong way—the devil's way. Jesus wouldn't do it. God's righteous words are more important than food. That was the right thing for Jesus to say and do.

> And the devil took him up and showed him all the kingdoms of the world in a moment of time, and said to him, "To you I will give all this authority and their glory, for it has been delivered to me, and I give it to whom I will. If you, then, will worship me, it will all be yours." And Jesus answered him, "It is written,
>
> > 'You shall worship the Lord your God,
> > and him only shall you serve.'" (Luke 4:5–8)

No matter what the devil promised, Jesus loved His Father most of all—more than all the riches of the world. Jesus answered again with God's righteous command. Jesus said and did what was right. After this, the devil tempted Jesus a third time, but again Jesus said and did what was right. In fact, from His birth in the manger until He returned to heaven, Jesus always said and did what was right in every situation. Just like His Father, Jesus is perfectly righteous. That is why Jesus is called the "Righteous One" (Acts 3:14).

Why is it important to know that God is righteous? Because God created you in His image and likeness (Genesis 1:27). That means you are to be *like* God in certain ways. You are to be like God in "true righteousness" (Ephesians 4:24). Imagine that God is like a beautiful treasure chest filled with priceless, dazzling gems. Would God want His people looking like ugly, stinky garbage? Of course not! A righteous God wants His people to be righteous too.

> For the LORD is righteous;
> he loves righteous deeds;
>> the upright shall behold his face. (Psalm 11:7)

LEARNING TO TRUST GOD

✦ Read Psalm 19:9 and Romans 7:12 again. What is your attitude toward God's righteous rules and commands? Do you *always* obey commands like "Honor your father and mother"? When tempted, do you always say and do the right thing like Jesus did? Why not? What does this tell you about yourself? Do you know any verses that explain this problem?

✦ Even as a little boy, Jesus never thought, said, or did anything wrong. Jesus is perfectly righteous—always and forever. Why is this good news for you? Read and talk about Hebrews 4:15 and 2 Corinthians 5:21.

✦ *Activity:* Make a Bible memory puzzle. On a large piece of stiff paper, write out Psalm 11:7. Decorate the paper along the edges. Then cut the paper into ten to twenty puzzle pieces of various shapes. Mix up the pieces and see how quickly you can assemble the puzzle. Recite the verse.

God Is Wrathful

Do you have a piggy bank or a special place to keep your money? Pretend for a minute that you had one hundred dollars stored inside a bank. Now imagine that someone came and stole the money. Would that be right? Why not? Would it be right for the person to be punished for stealing? Yes. There should be consequences for wrong actions.

In the last chapter, we learned that God is righteous. We also learned that God has given us His righteous rules and commands to follow and obey. They tell us what thoughts, feelings, words, and actions are right and pleasing to God. But what happens when people do not follow and obey God's commands? What happens when people do what is wrong instead? Would God be right to punish them in some way? Let's first look at a story from the Bible.

> The Passover of the Jews was at hand, and Jesus went up to Jerusalem. In the temple he found those who were selling oxen and sheep and pigeons, and the money-changers sitting there. And making a whip of cords, he drove them all out of the temple, with the sheep and oxen. And he poured out the coins of the money-changers and overturned their tables. And he told those who sold the pigeons, "Take these things away; do not make my Father's house a house of trade." (John 2:13–16)

The temple was the special place where God's people would go to meet together, worship, and pray. It was a sacred and holy place. But some people were using it like a store and selling animals to make money. They treasured making money more than they treasured God. They were not obeying the commandment "You shall love the LORD your God with all your heart and with all your soul and with all your might" (Deuteronomy 6:5). How would you describe Jesus's response?

Was Jesus right to respond this way? Yes. Jesus is perfectly righteous. He said and did the right thing. But this is just a tiny glimpse of God's righteous anger.

In the Old Testament, during the time of Abraham, there were two cities named Sodom and Gomorrah. The people in these cities did not follow and obey God's righteous rules and commands. They were extremely wicked. After giving them many opportunities to repent and turn away from their sinful ways, God decided it was the right time to punish them and give them the judgment they rightly deserved. Here is what happened:

> Then the LORD rained on Sodom and Gomorrah sulfur and fire from the LORD out of heaven. And he overthrew those cities, and all the valley, and all the inhabitants of the cities, and what grew on the ground. (Genesis 19:24–25)

We could look at many more examples of God's anger throughout the Bible. God has righteous anger when people do not treasure Him most of all. God is right to punish those who do not obey His righteous commands. The Bible uses a special word to describe God's anger: *wrath*.

His wrath is poured out like fire,
> and the rocks are broken into pieces by him. (Nahum 1:6)

For the wrath of God is revealed from heaven against all ungodliness and unrighteousness of men. (Romans 1:18)

God's anger is very fierce and terrible. That is what "wrath" is. God's wrath is His righteous anger at all "unrighteousness"—sin.

God is WRATHFUL—He is very angry at sin and is right to punish sinners.

But even as terrible as God's punishment on Sodom and Gomorrah was, there is another way that God shows just how much anger He has against sin. What could that be?

They will suffer the punishment of eternal destruction, away from the presence of the Lord and from the glory of his might. (2 Thessalonians 1:9)

This is a description of hell—a real place where unrighteous sinners will experience God's wrath forever. God has decided that this is the right punishment for unrighteous sinners. Nothing is more terrible or awful than this.

And God's wrath is not only for really bad and wicked people. It is "against all . . . unrighteousness"—all sins, both big and small. Why is this important to know? Think carefully about the following verses:

None is righteous, no, not one. (Romans 3:10)

For all have sinned and fall short of the glory of God. (Romans 3:23)

These verses are describing all of us, including you. Because you are also an unrighteous sinner, what do you deserve? God's righteous wrath! This is really bad news, and it is your biggest problem. It can't be solved by anything you can do. You are helpless. How should this make you feel about your sin? What would be the right way to respond to a wrathful God?

[God] commands all people everywhere to repent, because he has fixed a day on which he will judge the world in righteousness by a man whom he has appointed. (Acts 17:30–31)

Here is the good and amazing news for all who repent:

For God has not destined us for wrath, but to obtain salvation through our Lord Jesus Christ. (1 Thessalonians 5:9)

LEARNING TO TRUST GOD

✤ When you think about Jesus, what kinds of things come to mind? Do you think of His wrath against sin? How do Jesus's words and actions in the temple serve as a warning? Do you take God's wrath seriously? What's the only way to escape the righteous wrath of God?

✤ Would loving parents be right to be very angry if someone tried to hurt their child on purpose? Yes, love hates what is evil and is right to be angry at evil. In a similar way, God shows His love by hating what is evil. His wrath against sin is like a protection that guards what is good and right. It hates anything that would draw us away from the true, lasting joy that is found in Him alone.

✤ *Activity:* Continue adding to your set of flash cards (which you started in "God Is Omniscient"). Create flash cards for "God is Good," "God is Jealous," "God is Righteous," and "God is Wrathful."

God Is Patient

Have you ever become impatient when something didn't happen fast enough? Maybe it was a long car ride to somewhere fun, and you kept asking, "When are we going to get there? How much longer?" Or maybe it seems like it's taking forever for your birthday to arrive. Sometimes we just want things to happen quickly. But are there times when you would rather not have something happen quickly? Would you want your parents to be quick in giving you more chores or quick to become angry at you for not cleaning your room?

And would you want *this* to happen right away?

> The wrath of God is revealed from heaven against all ungodliness and unrighteousness of men. (Romans 1:18)

In the last chapter, we learned that God is wrathful. He is right to be angry at sin, and He is right to punish sinners. But is God quick to get angry? Is He quick to punish sinners? Does God get impatient with sinners and have a kind of temper tantrum when they sin? Those are all good and important questions. Where will we find the answers? Yes, in the Bible.

Let's look back long ago to the time in which Noah lived. Here is what the world was like:

> The LORD saw that the wickedness of man was great in the earth, and that every intention of the thoughts of his heart was only evil continually. And the LORD regretted that he had made man on the earth, and it grieved him to his heart. So the LORD said, "I will blot out man whom I have created from the face of the land, man and animals and creeping things and birds of the heavens, for I am sorry that I have made them." (Genesis 6:5–7)

The earth was filled with thousands upon thousands of very wicked people who were always intent on doing evil. They were people who rightly deserved God's righteous wrath. God was going to send a worldwide flood to destroy them and every living thing on earth. There was an exception, however: "Noah found favor in the eyes of the LORD" (Genesis 6:8). Unlike the other people, Noah was a man who loved and trusted God. So, God commanded Noah and his family to build an ark so that they could escape God's righteous judgment.

But do you know how long God waited until He sent the flood? From the time God told Noah to build the ark, God waited one hundred years to send the flood. That is a very long time! God was *slow* in bringing the promised destruction. During these long years,

- Noah worked on building the ark. (After all, it was a huge project!)
- Noah was a "herald of righteousness" (2 Peter 2:5)—he warned the people of God's coming judgment so that they might repent and turn away from their sins and trust in God.
- The wicked continued to work, sleep, eat, gather with friends, build houses, play, travel, and more.
- The wicked continued to ignore God and rebel against Him.

The wicked must have thought that God's promised judgment was a joke. Year after year they probably mocked Noah by saying, "Where's the flood? Did God forget?" They thought the "slowness" of the flood's coming meant that God's judgment wasn't real, so they continued in their wicked ways. But God's "slowness" was for a very special purpose.

> The Lord is not slow to fulfill his promise as some count slowness, but is patient toward you, not wishing that any should perish, but that all should reach repentance. (2 Peter 3:9)

God is not quick to get angry—He never has temper tantrums. He is not quick to punish either. He is a patient God.

God is PATIENT—He is slow to anger and slow to punish.

God is patient and wants to give sinners time to repent and turn from their wicked ways. Did the wicked people of Noah's day have enough time to repent? Of course they did. But in all that time, they did not repent. So God, who is always faithful in keeping His promises, revealed His wrath at just the right time and destroyed them. They had no excuse. God had been extremely patient with them. What about Noah? Because God was slow to send the flood, Noah and his family had enough time to complete the ark, and they were saved just as God promised.

> The LORD is gracious and merciful,
> slow to anger and abounding in steadfast love. (Psalm 145:8)

Why is it good for you that God is a patient God? Because from the time you started to grow inside your mother, you have had a sin "nature." This is proven every day as you sin against God in different ways. This is true of all of us. God would be right to punish us in His wrath immediately—so it's a very good thing that God is patient. But God's patience should not be toyed with. We should never think that we can guess how long God's patience will last before He brings judgment. He wants you to repent now and turn away from your sin. He wants you to trust in Jesus. He wants you to come to salvation and escape His wrath.

> Do you presume on the riches of his kindness and forbearance and patience, not knowing that God's kindness is meant to lead you to repentance? But because of your hard and impenitent heart you are storing up wrath for yourself on the day of wrath when God's righteous judgment will be revealed. (Romans 2:4–5)

LEARNING TO TRUST GOD

✠ How have you experienced God's patience this week? Have you sinned this week? But have you still been able to experience good things like food, family, friends, and play? Have you thanked God for His patience? Have you seen God's patience as an opportunity for you to repent of your sin and trust in Jesus?

✠ Patience is one of those attributes that God shares with us. That means He wants us to be patient too. Read and talk about Colossians 3:12–14 and James 1:19–20. Have you been impatient with someone this week? What would God want you to do?

✠ *Activity:* Play the Ark Game. Draw a picture of Noah's ark on a piece of stiff paper. Cut it into five or six separate pieces. Have a parent or sibling hide the pieces. Next, set a timer for ten minutes. Then, as quickly as possible, find the pieces and put them together to complete the ark before the "flood" comes (the timer runs out). Play it again, but decrease the amount of time allowed.

God Is Merciful

Have you ever received a surprise even though it wasn't a special occasion like your birthday? You could say that it was an "undeserved kindness"—meaning you didn't earn or win it. But do you realize that you receive hundreds of gifts of "undeserved kindness" every day?

> The LORD is good to all,
>> and his mercy is over all that he has made. (Psalm 145:9)

In a previous chapter, we learned that God is good to everyone. God gives to all people good things such as food, family, friends, homes, parks, pets, and more. All these things are "undeserved kindnesses" from God. They are gifts. We do not deserve any of these good things. But God in His mercy gives these good things. God's mercy is His kindness to people who don't deserve it. Why don't we deserve God's kindness? Because we are all unrighteous sinners. What we all *deserve* is God's righteous wrath and punishment. That is terrible news. But does God show kindness to undeserving sinners?

> You are a God ready to forgive, gracious and merciful, slow to anger and abounding in steadfast love. (Nehemiah 9:17)

Even though all of us deserve God's wrath because of our sin, God stands ready and willing to forgive us. That is because **God is MERCIFUL—He is kind to undeserving sinners.**

God's mercy is a gift because it is something we didn't deserve and could not earn. In His mercy, God gladly forgives sinners who come to Him with hearts that are truly humble and sorry. That is the best kindness of all!

In the Bible, Jesus told a parable that describes this kind of amazing mercy. (A parable is a make-believe story that is meant to teach us true things about God and ourselves.) Here is the story:

There was a man who had two sons. And the younger of them said to his father, "Father, give me the share of property that is coming to me." And he divided his property between them. Not many days later, the younger son gathered all he had and took a journey into a far country, and there he squandered his property in reckless living. And when he had spent everything, a severe famine arose in that country, and he began to be in need. So he went and hired himself out to one of the citizens of that country, who sent him into his fields to feed pigs. And he was longing to be fed with the pods that the pigs ate, and no one gave him anything. (Luke 15:11–16)

Think about it: For a son to ask for his share of his father's property was very disrespectful. It was like saying, "I'd rather have your money than be with you." When the father kindly gave his son the money, did the son spend it doing good things? Not at all! Did the son's way of doing things make him happy in the end? No, he went from enjoying the love and goodness of his father to being envious of what pigs had to eat! But finally, the son had a change of heart. He realized that doing things his own way did not bring him happiness. He realized how loving and good his father was, and he understood that he had sinned greatly against his father. He decided to return to his father and humbly beg for forgiveness.

But how would his father respond? Did this sinful son *deserve* his father's forgiveness? No, he didn't. But here is what happened:

> But while he was still a long way off, his father saw him and felt compassion, and ran and embraced him and kissed him. . . . "For this my son was dead, and is alive again; he was lost, and is found." And they began to celebrate. (Luke 15:20, 24)

In this parable, who do you think the father is like—us or God? Who is the son like—us or God? Just like the son, we have all sinned. We have failed to love and treasure God most of all. We want to do things our own way even though it leads to misery in the end—the eternal misery of hell. But what is God showing us about Himself through this story? Did the father turn his son away or tell him that he had to earn back the money he had given him first? No. That is because,

> when the goodness and loving kindness of God our Savior appeared, he saved us, not because of works done by us in righteousness, but according to his own mercy. (Titus 3:4–5)

So, how should a person respond to God's mercy? Would it be right to reject it or to receive it humbly and gladly?

To you, O Lord, I cry,
    and to the Lord I plead for mercy:

. . . .

"Hear, O Lord, and be merciful to me!
    O Lord, be my helper!" (Psalm 30:8, 10)

LEARNING TO TRUST GOD

✛ Read Psalm 145:9 again. Think about the hundreds of ways that God is kind to all people. How has God shown mercy even to wicked people? When someone gives you an undeserved gift, what is the right way to respond? Do you give thanks to God for His mercy?

✛ Have you ever received mercy from your parents when you deserved to be punished for something? How does it feel to receive "undeserved kindness"? Do you understand why you need the saving mercy of God—the kind of mercy that saves you from God's wrath? Read and talk about Titus 3:4–5 and Psalm 30:8, 10.

✛ *Activity:* Find a gift bag or decorate a small, open box with gift wrap. Cut out small slips of paper. Place the bag or box and the slips of paper on your dinner table. Before dinner, have each person who is eating with you write out a mercy he or she has received from God that day. Put these slips in the bag or box. Then spend a few minutes in prayer thanking God for His mercy. Do this for an entire week.

God Is the Deliverer

Have you ever carried a really heavy load? Maybe you had a heavy backpack, or maybe you gave another child a piggyback ride. Imagine carrying a big load like that all the time. And what if you tried to swim while carrying it? That would be really dangerous! You'd sink! In the Bible, God describes the people of Israel as being weighed down by sin (Isaiah 1:4). Sin is like a heavy weight that we carry around. It is dreary, distressing, dangerous, and deadly.

> The wrath of God comes upon the sons of disobedience. (Ephesians 5:6)

> The wages of sin is death. (Romans 6:23)

This wasn't just a problem for the people of Israel. Because of Adam and Eve's first sinful act in the garden of Eden, all people have *inherited* this problem (Romans 5:12, 19). We are also weighed down by sin. We all deserve God's wrath and righteous punishment. We deserve death. This is our biggest problem, and it's a problem that we are completely helpless to solve. What can be done?

> Turn, O Lord, deliver my life;
>   save me for the sake of your steadfast love. (Psalm 6:4)

> Deliver me from all my transgressions. (Psalm 39:8)

We need God to deliver us—to save us—from our sins. We need God to deliver us from His wrath and the punishment we deserve. So, before He even created the world, the eternal God—Father, Son, and Holy Spirit—made a loving, good, wise, and perfect plan to save sinners. God Himself would become the Deliverer, the

Savior, of His desperate people. That is why the Son of God came to earth as a real human baby and was named "Jesus," which means "Yahweh [the LORD] saves."

How did Jesus save and deliver God's people? Well, let's pretend for a minute that you are carrying a backpack weighed down with sin. Every sin of yours is like a heavy rock filling the backpack. You are "crushed" under the weight of all that sin, but you're not able to take it off. It's way too heavy! Now think of Jesus. Would He have any "weight of sin" of His own? No. Jesus is perfectly righteous. He never, ever sinned. Not even once! Because of this, Jesus was able to act as the Deliverer of God's people by becoming a "substitute" for them. Carefully read these verses to understand what Jesus did.

> Surely he has borne our griefs
>   and carried our sorrows. (Isaiah 53:4)

> He was pierced for our transgressions;
>   he was crushed for our iniquities. (Isaiah 53:5)

> The LORD has laid on him
>> the iniquity of us all. (Isaiah 53:6)

Or here's an easier way to say it:

> He himself bore our sins in his body on the tree. (1 Peter 2:24)

It's like Jesus took that heavy sin-filled backpack from you—and not just from you but from all God's people! And what did Jesus do with the heavy, awful sin of thousands upon thousands of people? He took it upon His own body on "the tree," meaning the cross. So Jesus was hanging on the cross, bearing the huge and enormous weight of sin. But the worst was yet to come because . . .

What does God feel toward sin? Fierce and terrible anger—wrath. What is the right punishment for sin? Death. So, while Jesus hung on the cross, God the Father poured out His fierce wrath on His own Son and punished Jesus to death. We cannot even begin to imagine how heartbreaking this must have been! Yet Jesus willingly received all the wrath and punishment His people deserved. And because He did, God will never, ever pour out His wrath and punishment on anyone who trusts in Jesus as his one and only Deliverer and Savior.

God is the DELIVERER—He saves His sinful people from the punishment they deserve.

But there is something else that Jesus did to deliver His people. Sinners don't simply need to have their sins taken away and punished once and for all; we also need to be *given* something in order to enjoy eternal life with a righteous God. When Jesus was raised from the dead, He showed that He was without sin and had a perfect righteousness—righteousness that He gives to His people.

> For our sake he made him to be sin who knew no sin, so that in him we might become the righteousness of God. (2 Corinthians 5:21)

Not having a righteousness of my own that comes from the law, but that which comes through faith in Christ, the righteousness from God that depends on faith. (Philippians 3:9)

This is the best news in the world! There is a solution to our biggest problem. God has made a way to deliver His people. This is the good news of the gospel: there is salvation in Jesus! How do you receive this salvation? Is it enough to simply "know about" what Jesus did? Do you receive salvation because you go to church and Sunday school? Here is what the Bible says you must do:

Repent and believe in the gospel. (Mark 1:15)

Believe in the Lord Jesus, and you will be saved. (Acts 16:31)

LEARNING TO TRUST GOD

✦ Do you ever feel the "weight" of your own sin? (Maybe you feel guilt, shame, helplessness, etc.) Why is Jesus the only one who can deliver us and save us? Have you called upon Him with sincere sorrow for your sin and true belief in what He has done for you?

✦ How do we know that what Jesus did on the cross truly saves and delivers sinners who trust in Him? Is there any "proof" that Jesus saves His people from sin and death and gives them eternal life? Read and talk about 1 Peter 1:3–5.

✦ *Activity:* With your parents' help, find the words and music to the hymn "In Christ Alone" by Keith Getty and Stuart Townend. Read and talk about the words, and then sing it together.

God Is Holy

Have you ever seen or experienced something so awesome that it took your breath away? (Maybe a giant roller coaster?) Or maybe it was something so overwhelmingly powerful that it left you trembling? Or maybe it was something so beautiful that you just wanted to sit and admire it? After seeing or experiencing those kinds of things, you may have found it difficult to even describe them to others. They were just too amazing!

Long ago, the prophet Isaiah had a one-of-a-kind, beyond-imagination experience. He saw something that . . . well, let's just read exactly what happened.

> I saw the Lord sitting upon a throne, high and lifted up; and the train of his robe filled the temple. Above him stood the seraphim. Each had six wings: with two he covered his face, and with two he covered his feet, and with two he flew. And one called to another and said:
>
> > "Holy, holy, holy is the LORD of hosts;
> > the whole earth is full of his glory!"
>
> And the foundations of the thresholds shook at the voice of him who called, and the house was filled with smoke. (Isaiah 6:1–4)

This was no ordinary thing to see or experience! Isaiah *saw* God, the Lord of hosts, on His great throne. Isaiah **experienced** being in His presence. And when the Lord of hosts spoke, His voice was so powerful that the ground shook. Even the heavenly seraphim (angelic beings) covered their faces because the sight of God was too dazzling to behold. Being in His presence was like nothing else. That is why the seraphim called out, "Holy, holy, holy is the LORD of hosts." What does the word *holy* mean? Here is a verse that will help us to understand:

To whom then will you compare me,
   that I should be like him? says the Holy One. (Isaiah 40:25)

God is asking whether there is anything that you could compare to Him. So, for example, could Isaiah have come away saying something like "I saw the Lord and was in His presence, and it was like the time I saw a really terrific thunderstorm"? Not at all! Consider for a minute who God is and what He is like: Incomprehensible, Eternal, Glorious, Wise, Almighty, Sovereign, Self-Sufficient, Faithful, a Trinity, Happy, Love, Omnipresent, Unchanging, Omniscient, Good, Jealous, Righteous, Wrathful, Patient, Merciful, and the only Deliverer. God is beyond comparison. He is one of a kind and totally unique. He is like nothing else and is separate from all other things or beings. This is what *holy* means, and that is why God calls Himself the "Holy One."

How do you think Isaiah responded to being in the presence of the holy God? He said,

> Woe is me! For I am lost; for I am a man of unclean lips, and I dwell in the midst of a people of unclean lips; for my eyes have seen the King, the LORD of hosts! (Isaiah 6:5)

Isaiah felt afraid, lost, and ruined. Why? Being in the presence of a holy God made Isaiah realize how "unclean"—desperately sinful—he was. That is because God's holiness not only means that He is one of a kind and separate from all other things. It also means that God is completely separate from sin. God is perfect and pure. (Think of a perfectly clear and spotless window, for example.)

God is HOLY—He is like nothing else. He is perfect and separate from sin.

As a holy God, He cannot tolerate sin or look at it and say it doesn't matter (Habakkuk 1:13). That is why Isaiah responded the way he did. That is why, just like us, Isaiah needed a Deliverer, a Savior. And so Jesus came so that we could come into God's holy presence and not be lost.

So how should we respond to a holy God? Well, imagine for a moment that you were given a large, priceless, brilliant diamond. Would you simply throw it into a junk drawer? Would you use it instead of a baseball and hit it with a bat? Would you trade it with a friend for his new video game? Of course not! Now think of the holy God. A diamond cannot compare to His greatness and worth! So how should we treat a holy God? For example, ask yourself . . .

- Is it right to treat God's Holy Word—the Bible—like just another book? Or to toss it around and treat it like a toy?
- Is it right to act silly or uninterested when God's people gather together to worship Him?
- Is it right to act as if disobeying your parents or fighting with your siblings isn't really a big deal to a holy God?

Because God is holy, we should be in awe of Him more than of anything else. He deserves to be treated with the highest honor and respect. He deserves our worship.

> Splendor and majesty are before him;
>> strength and beauty are in his sanctuary.

. . . .

> Worship the LORD in the splendor of holiness;
>> tremble before him, all the earth!

> Say among the nations, "The LORD reigns!" (Psalm 96:6, 9–10)

LEARNING TO TRUST GOD

✤ Do you treat God as one of a kind and beyond comparison to anything or anyone else? Why are our hearts sometimes drawn to see other things as more awesome than God? What could help your awe of God to grow?

✤ Read and talk about 1 Peter 1:15–16. Why is it important for God's people to be holy—"set apart" from sin and following in His holy ways? Can we become holy without trusting in Jesus? Why not? (See Colossians 1:21–22.) What "tools" and help has God given His people so that they might grow in holiness? (See John 14:26 and 17:17.)

✤ *Activity:* Make a "God Is Holy" Bible bookmark. Using stiff, durable paper, cut out a rectangle measuring about two inches by seven inches. Write "God is Holy" in large letters across the length of it. Decorate it to make it look very special. Use it as a bookmark for your Bible.

God Is Worthy

Suppose you saved up your money and bought a brand-new bicycle for seventy dollars. The next day, a friend came over with his old, rusty bike to see your new one. He offered to trade his old bike for your new one. Would that be a good trade? Why not? But what if someone came and said, "I'll trade you ten thousand dollars for your new bike." Why would that be a great trade?

In the Bible, Jesus told two very short parables about two men who made great trades. The stories are meant to point us to a type of trade—the best trade of all. What could that be?

> The kingdom of heaven is like treasure hidden in a field, which a man found and covered up. Then in his joy he goes and sells all that he has and buys that field.
>
> Again, the kingdom of heaven is like a merchant in search of fine pearls, who, on finding one pearl of great value, went and sold all that he had and bought it. (Matthew 13:44–46)

In these stories, two men are willing to sell everything they own (make a trade) in order to receive something even better. Jesus compares their good trades—for the treasure in a field and the pearl of great value—to the kingdom of heaven. What does that mean? . . . Well, let's look at two true stories about men who actually did something just like the men in Jesus's parables.

> While walking by the Sea of Galilee, he saw two brothers, Simon (who is called Peter) and Andrew his brother, casting a net into the sea, for they were fishermen. And he said to them, "Follow me, and I will make you fishers of men." Immediately they left their nets and followed him. And

going on from there he saw two other brothers, James the son of Zebedee and John his brother, in the boat with Zebedee their father, mending their nets, and he called them. Immediately they left the boat and their father and followed him. (Matthew 4:18–22)

After this he went out and saw a tax collector named Levi [also referred to as Matthew], sitting at the tax booth. And he said to him, "Follow me." And leaving everything, he rose and followed him. (Luke 5:27–28)

The five men in these true stories left behind everything to follow someone. Who was that someone? Jesus. Why would they do this? Because they rightly understood that Jesus was more valuable and precious than all their worldly possessions, even their jobs and families. Jesus was *worth* giving up everything else for! Here is how another follower of Jesus explained it:

Indeed, I count everything as loss because of the surpassing worth of knowing Christ Jesus my Lord. For his sake I have suffered the loss of all things and count them as rubbish, in order that I may gain Christ. (Philippians 3:8)

These words were written by the apostle Paul. Paul knew that knowing and following Jesus was of "surpassing worth"—that means of "greatest worth." Think of how important and valuable your family and friends are to you. Jesus is millions of times more important and millions of times more valuable! Everything else, even the good things God has given us, cannot compare to how much He is worth.

So how should we act toward God? What would show that we truly believe He is worth more than anything else? Let's look at three ways.

First, because God is most valuable, He deserves our greatest love. Just think how much James and John loved their father. Think of how much you love your own parents. Jesus deserves to be loved more!

> And you shall love the Lord your God with all your heart and with all your soul and with all your mind and with all your strength. (Mark 12:30)

Second, because God is most valuable, He also deserves our obedience. That is why when Jesus called to the men and said, "Follow me," they obeyed.

> If you love me, you will keep my commandments. (John 14:15)

Third, because God is most valuable, He deserves our worship. That means our greatest admiration, awe, and respect should be for God. Our loudest cheering and clapping should be for God. Our best singing and praises should be for God. We should always recognize and feel that God is worth more to us than everything else in the whole world.

God is WORTHY—He is most valuable and deserves our greatest love, obedience, and worship.

> Let us be grateful for receiving a kingdom that cannot be shaken, and thus let us offer to God acceptable worship, with reverence and awe. (Hebrews 12:28)

John (the fisherman who left everything to follow Jesus) was given a glimpse of God's throne room in heaven. He wrote about it in the book of Revelation, the last book of the Bible. What did he see there? Too many heavenly creatures to count were loudly saying,

Worthy is the Lamb who was slain,
to receive power and wealth and wisdom and might
and honor and glory and blessing! (Revelation 5:12)

LEARNING TO TRUST GOD

✠ Pretend you found a treasure chest filled with gold. What would you do with it? Why? Do you see Jesus as more valuable than anything else? In what ways has He shown that He is worthy of your greatest love, obedience, and worship?

✠ If Jesus is worth more to you than anything else, how will this be shown in your life? How can reading the Bible every day help you to see Him as more and more valuable? How can praying every day to Him help you?

✠ *Activity:* With your parents' help, play the "What's it worth?" guessing game. Choose various items from around your house that you especially enjoy. After picking each item ask, "What's it worth?" Give your own guess, and then have your parents give you their answer (just an estimate). Then say the refrain "Jesus is worth much, much more!" When you're done, talk about Philippians 3:8.

God Is Bountiful

Have you ever run out of something or not had enough of it? For example, maybe you and your mom decided to make your favorite cookies. But when you started scooping flour into the mixing bowl, you realized there was not enough flour. You had run out. What a disappointment! Or suppose you and your dad are building a tree house, but halfway through the project you realize you don't have enough wood to complete it. Another disappointment! That's just the way things are sometimes.

The Bible tells a story about people who did not have enough of something important. Here is what happened:

> In those days, when again a great crowd had gathered, and they had nothing to eat, he called his disciples to him and said to them, "I have compassion on the crowd, because they have been with me now three days and have nothing to eat. And if I send them away hungry to their homes, they will faint on the way. And some of them have come from far away." And his disciples answered him, "How can one feed these people with bread here in this desolate place?" And he asked them, "How many loaves do you have?" They said, "Seven." (Mark 8:1–5)

There were about four thousand really hungry people and only seven loaves of bread—definitely not enough. How extremely disappointing that would be! But Jesus was not done yet.

> He directed the crowd to sit down on the ground. And he took the seven loaves, and having given thanks, he broke them and gave them to his disciples to set before the people; and they set them before the crowd. And

they had a few small fish. And having blessed them, he said that these also should be set before them. And they ate and were satisfied. And they took up the broken pieces left over, seven baskets full. (Mark 8:6–8)

How was Jesus able to make all that food from seven loaves and a few fish? He is almighty God. But did Jesus provide "just enough" food? No, He provided more than enough—and because He did, everyone was "satisfied." They were so full that they couldn't eat another bite. That is why there were leftovers. But this story isn't only about Jesus providing people with more than enough food to eat. It also shows us something even more important about God.

Jesus said to them, "I am the bread of life; whoever comes to me shall not hunger, and whoever believes in me shall never thirst." (John 6:35)

What did Jesus mean by this? Here are some verses that will help to explain what Jesus meant:

In him we have redemption through his blood, the forgiveness of our trespasses, according to the riches of his grace, which he lavished upon us. (Ephesians 1:7–8)

. . . so that in the coming ages he might show the immeasurable riches of his grace in kindness toward us in Christ Jesus. (Ephesians 2:7)

And my God will supply every need of yours according to his riches in glory in Christ Jesus. (Philippians 4:19)

After reading these verses, would you say that God is *just* enough to meet the needs of His people? No. God is *more* than enough. Is He enough to meet only some needs but not others? No. God is able to meet and satisfy all our deepest needs and desires. Will He ever run out and disappoint His people? No, the eternal and self-sufficient God will *always and forever* be more than enough for His people. That is because **God is BOUNTIFUL—He is more than enough to satisfy all our desires.**

Think for a minute of a spring of water. A spring is a source of water that comes up from the ground all by itself. It's like a fountain that never runs out of water. The water just keeps coming and coming. God calls Himself the "fountain of living waters" (Jeremiah 2:13). This can help us to understand what it means that God is bountiful. His goodness, love, power, faithfulness, wisdom, patience, mercy, happiness, and righteousness are like a never-ending source of water. Because God is bountiful, He just keeps pouring out Himself for His people, but He never ever runs out; He is always more than enough.

So how should you respond to this bountiful God who is more than enough to satisfy all your desires?

I will sing to the LORD,
   because he has dealt bountifully with me. (Psalm 13:6)

Bless the LORD, O my soul,
   and all that is within me,
   bless his holy name!
Bless the LORD, O my soul,
   and forget not all his benefits. (Psalm 103:1–2)

LEARNING TO TRUST GOD

✛ In what ways has God been bountiful to you? Does the fact that God is bountiful mean that He will give us everything we *want*? What does He promise to give His people? Do you pray and humbly ask to receive more of His goodness in your life? How can you show thanks to God this week for His bountiful provision?

✛ Have you ever considered why God made us with a hunger for food? What do you crave and seek when you're really hungry? What does it feel like when you have a full tummy? How can this help you to better understand your need for what God bountifully provides? How is the satisfaction that Jesus brings better than any food?

✛ *Activity:* Draw or construct a pretend water fountain. You could use strips of blue construction paper and curl them to look like streams of water coming up out of the fountain you've made. Write one of the following on each of the streams of water: Goodness, Love, Power, Faithfulness, Wisdom, Patience, Mercy, Happiness, and Righteousness. At the bottom of the fountain, write "The Eternal God is Bountiful."

Two More Questions

In the very first chapter of this book, you were introduced to the two most important questions of all: *Who is God?* and *What is God like?* By looking at God's Word, you have discovered answers—not every answer, but enough to give you a better understanding of the greatness and worth of God. There was also another important question that came after the first two: *How should I act toward God?* You discovered that you should do things like trust, love, praise, obey, worship, follow, believe, and honor God. Now let's look at two more questions: *Who are you?* and *What are you to be like?*

Let's see what the Bible says about the question *Who are you?*

So God created man in his own image,
>   in the image of God he created him;
>   male and female he created them. (Genesis 1:27)

You are God's image bearer. God created you in His own likeness with special characteristics and abilities that are similar to His. That is why you, and all other people, are more special than all the stars, mountains, oceans, plants, animals, and other created things. You have a mind that can think and know God. You have a heart that can love and enjoy God. You have a will that can trust and obey God. The reason God created you this way is for *His glory* (Psalm 86:9–12). That means you are to think, feel, and act in ways that always show that God is most special—He is the greatest and best! Who are you? You are an image bearer of God, created in His likeness for His glory.

Now let's look at some answers from the Bible about our second question: *What are you to be like?*

Hear instruction and be wise. (Proverbs 8:33)

Be strong in the Lord. (Ephesians 6:10)

You also, be patient. (James 5:8)

Be merciful, even as your Father is merciful. (Luke 6:36)

Be holy in all your conduct. (1 Peter 1:15)

Abhor what is evil; hold fast to what is good. (Romans 12:9)

Be glad in the LORD. (Psalm 32:11)

Be kind to one another, tenderhearted, forgiving one another. (Ephesians 4:32)

Be generous and ready to share. (1 Timothy 6:18)

Hmm . . . a lot of these words look familiar, don't they? They are words we've used to describe God: wise, strong, patient, merciful, holy, good, glad (happy), and more. So are you to actually *be like God*?

Put on the new self, created after the likeness of God in true righteousness and holiness. (Ephesians 4:24)

Therefore be imitators of God, as beloved children. (Ephesians 5:1)

To be an "imitator of God" means to "take after" Him. How? By looking to and taking after His Son. God wants you to *be like Jesus* (Romans 8:29). You are to take after Jesus by setting your mind on what is true and right. You are to have a heart that loves as He does. You are to follow His example and walk in obedience. Do you think that's easy to do? Read the verses on the previous page and ask yourself, "Do I always act wisely? Am I always kind? Do I ever get impatient when things don't go my way?" Think of an "imitator" again. Not everything is able to be an "imitator." For example, a rock could never imitate a person's words or actions. That would be impossible for a rock to do. Now look at the "rock" in this verse.

And I will give you a new heart, and a new spirit I will put within you. And I will remove the heart of stone from your flesh and give you a heart of flesh. (Ezekiel 36:26)

All people are born with hearts that are like rock—sinful hearts. It's impossible for you to be an imitator of God unless He acts to give you a new heart—a heart of flesh. And that is exactly what the Holy Spirit does for God's people. When the Holy Spirit does this, something amazing happens—He makes a person "born again" (John 3:3) and "alive" (Ephesians 2:5) to Christ. That means that a person begins to hate sin and wants to turn away from it and run to Jesus for forgiveness. (That's what repentance is.) A person then believes in Jesus and depends on Him as the one and only Savior. (That's what faith is.) That is why Jesus calls you to "repent and believe" (Mark 1:15). This is your only hope for being what God wants you to be. You need Jesus!

But to all who did receive him, who believed in his name, he gave the right to become children of God. (John 1:12)

There is one final verse for us to look at as we answer *What are you to be like?* It is a verse that talks about some very special privileges God's beloved children enjoy, and it also tells of a very special responsibility they have.

> But you are a chosen race, a royal priesthood, a holy nation, a people for his own possession, that you may proclaim the excellencies of him who called you out of darkness into his marvelous light. (1 Peter 2:9)

What "excellencies" are God's beloved children supposed to proclaim and tell others about? Well, here are a few: God is incomprehensible, eternal, glorious, wise, almighty, sovereign, self-sufficient, faithful, a Trinity, happy, love, omnipresent, unchanging, omniscient, good, jealous, righteous, wrathful, patient, merciful, the Deliverer, holy, worthy, and bountiful!

Go and tell everyone in the world about the greatness and worth of God!

LEARNING TO TRUST GOD

✤ Do you see your true need for Jesus? How is this shown in your life? Why can't you do what you were created to do without Him? Why do you need the Holy Spirit's help? Read and talk about Psalm 86:9–12.

✤ Even for those who repent and believe, becoming like Jesus is a process. It doesn't happen all at once. But God has given His children everything they need to do this. Read and talk about Matthew 6:9–13; John 14:26; Ephesians 4:11–13; and 2 Timothy 3:14–17.

✤ *Activity:* Complete your set of God's Attribute flash cards. How does each attribute of God show one of His "excellencies"? With your parents' help, think about how you could share some of these truths about God with a friend or family member this week.

Truth78 Partners with Parents and Churches

Truth78 is a vision-oriented ministry for the next generations—that they may know, honor, and treasure God, setting their hope in Christ alone, so that they will live as faithful disciples for the glory of God. Our mission is to inspire and equip the church and the home for the comprehensive discipleship of the next generations.

Truth78 offers a number of resources for parents and churches, including the following titles:

Curricula

God's Attributes was adapted from The ABCs of God, an elementary-age curriculum published by Truth78 that is one of twenty-seven curricula for use with children from birth through the teen years.

Family Devotionals

More Than a Story takes children from ages six through twelve on a chronological journey through the Bible with a God-centered, gospel-focused, discipleship-oriented, theologically grounded perspective. Available in two volumes that cover the Old Testament and the New Testament, these books are illustrated in full color.

Glorious God, Glorious Gospel: An Interactive Family Devotional was developed for parents to use with their children to ground them in the essential, foundational, and glorious truths of the gospel. An accompanying notebook and coloring book engage and equip young minds.

Discipleship Booklets

True behavior change comes through the heart-transforming work of regeneration through faith in Christ and the enabling power of the Holy Spirit. Learning Christ: Putting off the Old, Putting on the New is a new series of booklets for parents and those who counsel or instruct children and youth.

Learn how to discern stages of spiritual growth, communicate the essential truths of the gospel, prepare the hearts of children to hear the gospel, and present the gospel in an accurate and child-friendly manner. *Helping Children to Understand the Gospel* includes a ten-week family devotional.

Each blessing explored in *A Father's Guide to Blessing His Children* is based upon a biblical text and flows from a father's heart for his daughters and a pastor's heart for the next generations.

Mothers: Disciplers of the Next Generations will challenge you to look at mothering with a biblical perspective, to daily seize opportunities to encourage faith in your children, and to rely on Him to accomplish the great work to which He has called you.

The Greatest Treasure is a small booklet providing ten simple truth statements, each of which is accompanied by supporting Scriptures, a brief explanation and call for personal application, and an illustration that summarizes and reinforces it.

Children's Books

The Very Bad News & the Very Good News and *The World Created, Fallen, Redeemed, and Restored* provide a simple gospel presentation using the themes of creation, fall, redemption, and restoration to help children to understand and be able to explain to others the good news of the gospel.

When I Am Afraid gives parents the opportunity to show their children the wonderful promises of God and to encourage them to look to God when they are fearful.

My Church Notebooks

Church services give us the opportunity to come into the presence of God with other people of God, both young and old. As children observe and join believers in worship, they learn to concentrate on God and see His greatness. Three distinct church notebooks help children from three years old through elementary school to participate in their church services.

Scripture Memory Resources

Truth78's Fighter Verses™ Bible memory program is designed to encourage churches, families, and individuals in the lifelong practice and love of Bible memorization. The Fighter Verses program utilizes an easy-to-use Bible memory system with carefully chosen verses to help fight the good fight of faith. Available in print or app form. Foundation Verses resources provide seventy-six key verses for preschoolers to memorize, accompanied by full-color illustrations.

For more information on resources and training materials, please contact us.
Truth78.org | info@Truth78.org | (877) 400-1414 | @Truth78org